HARRY &
MEGHAN

HARRY &
MEGHAN
THE LOVE STORY

EMILY HERBERT

JOHN BLAKE

Published by John Blake Publishing,
3 Bramber Court, 2 Bramber Road,
London W14 9PB, England

www.johnblakebooks.com

www.facebook.com/johnblakebooks 🅵
twitter.com/jblakebooks 🅴

This edition published in 2017

ISBN: 978 1 78606 4 226

British Library Cataloguing-in-Publication Data:

A catalogue record for this book is available from the British Library.

Design by www.envydesign.co.uk

Printed and bound in Great Britain by Clays Ltd, St Ives plc

1 3 5 7 9 10 8 6 4 2

Papers used by John Blake Publishing are natural, recyclable products made from
wood grown in sustainable forests. The manufacturing processes conform to the
environmental regulations of the country of origin.

Every attempt has been made to contact the relevant copyright-holders, but some
were unobtainable. We would be grateful if the appropriate people could contact us.

John Blake Publishing is an imprint of Bonnier Publishing
www.bonnierpublishing.co.uk

CONTENTS

CHAPTER 1   PRINCESS MEGHAN   1

CHAPTER 2   A STAR IN THE MAKING   21

CHAPTER 3   DIPLOMATIC RELATIONS   41

CHAPTER 4   FAME AWAITS   57

CHAPTER 5   *SUITS*   75

CHAPTER 6   THE TIG   93

CHAPTER 7   THE CAMPAIGNER   107

CHAPTER 8   AN HEIR AND A SPARE   121

CHAPTER 9   CHILDHOOD'S END   137

CHAPTER 10   MILITARY MAN   153

CHAPTER 11   FIRST LOVE   171

CHAPTER 12   A SOLDIER AND A PRINCE   189

CHAPTER 13   CHRISTMAS IN KENSINGTON   207

CHAPTER 14   THE PITFALLS OF FAME   225

CHAPTER 15   HAPPY EVER AFTER?   241

CHAPTER 1

PRINCESS MEGHAN

It was the most hotly anticipated announcement in recent Royal history. Prince Harry was to marry his girlfriend of 18 months, the US actress Meghan Markle. The announcement came in that most modern of ways, via an announcement from Clarence House on Twitter:

'His Royal Highness the Prince of Wales is delighted to announce the engagement of Prince Harry to Ms. Meghan Markle. The wedding will take place in Spring 2018. Further details about the wedding day will be announced in due course. His Royal Highness and Ms Markle became engaged in London

earlier this month. Prince Harry has informed Her Majesty the Queen and other close members of his family. Prince Harry has also sought and received the blessing of Ms Markle's parents. The couple will live in Nottingham Cottage at Kensington Palace.'

A few hours later, the pair made a public appearance in the Sunken Garden at Kensington Palace, Meghan elegant in a white coat, showing off her ring. It had been designed by Harry himself, with two of Princess Diana's diamonds flaking a larger central diamond from Botswana, set on a gold band. 'When did Harry know she was the one?' a reporter asked. 'The first time we met,' Harry replied. Meghan was beaming. It was the happy ending the world had been waiting for ever since news of the relationship began to come out.

The couple had been keeping the world on tenterhooks for months, with 'will they won't they' speculation and certainly the advent of Meghan as a Royal bride was a huge indication of quite how much the Royal family had changed over the decades – and kept up with the times. The last time an American divorcee had captured the heart of a Windsor, it had ended up with the abdication of Edward VIII. This time round there was no problem at all, with Harry not losing his place in the line of succession. Although given that his father, aunt and one uncle were also divorcees it could hardly have been otherwise.

Instead, there was nothing but happiness and good wishes from the rest of the Windsors. The Queen, whose permission Harry had had to ask, and Duke of Edinburgh issued a statement saying they were 'delighted for the couple and wish them every happiness.' Harry's father, Prince Charles, said he was 'thrilled'. The Duke and Duchess of Cambridge said they were 'very excited for Meghan and Harry... It has been wonderful getting to know Meghan and to see how happy she and Harry are together.' The prime minister, Theresa May sent her 'very warmest congratulations' and wished them 'great happiness for the future'. And of course Meghan's own parents, Thomas Markle and Doria Ragland, had their own input, saying they were 'incredibly happy' and added, 'To see her union with Harry, who shares the same qualities, is a source of great joy for us'.

Matters had moved both slowly and fast. The couple's relationship had been confirmed a year earlier by none other than Harry himself, of which more below, but it had been less than two months since their first public appearance, at the Invictus Games in Toronto. It had also leaked out that the two had taken tea with the Queen, while Meghan had quit her role on the long-running television show in which she made her name, *Suits*. But most of the relationship had been conducted behind closed doors in London, Toronto and the various exotic locations to which Harry whisked his girlfriend, with information only gradually filtering out.

And Meghan was the first in almost every conceivable way for a Royal bride. She was an American, biracial actress who had already been married before. Her forebears on her mother's side had been slaves, a far cry from the members of European royalty and the British aristocracy, the breeding ground for many a Royal bride. Nor was her immediate background straightforward, with a cast of half-siblings commenting from the sidelines, sometimes in an extremely disobliging manner. But Meghan, like her sister-in-law to be Catherine Middleton had played a blinder, never referring to any family conflict, never badmouthing anyone. But she was no pushover either, proving equally willing to talk about the issues surrounding a mixed race identity. She was also, like Harry's late mother, a proven humanitarian, something which many speculated had drawn the two together. She had worked on a number of UN missions and crucially, as an actress, she was used to public scrutiny. She was certainly about to get enough of that.

Indeed, it was almost exactly one year earlier that the level of public scrutiny led Harry to issue an unprecedented and very personal statement asking that her privacy be respected, something no member of the Royal family had done before. It was long, informative, and confirmed something that until then had only been a rumour – and the tone was so impassioned and personal that it appeared to have been something composed in the heat of the moment, rather than laboured over by civil servants and issued in the more usual sombre prose. It was early November 2016 and it stunned Royal observers, who had never before seen its like. So what prompted this highly unusual document, parts of which are reproduced below?

Since he was young, Prince Harry has been very aware of the warmth that has been extended to him by members of the public. He feels lucky to have so many people supporting him and knows what a fortunate and privileged life he leads. He is also aware that there is significant curiosity about his private life. He has never been comfortable with this, but he has tried to develop a thick skin about the level of media interest that comes with it […] But the past week has seen a line crossed. His girlfriend, Meghan Markle, has

been subject to a wave of abuse and harassment [...]
Prince Harry is worried about Ms. Markle's safety and
is deeply disappointed that he has not been able to
protect her [...] He knows commentators will say this
is 'the price she has to pay' and that 'this is all part of
the game'. He strongly disagrees. This is not a game –
it is her life and his.

The statement purported to come from the Communications Secretary to Prince Harry, but to anyone who read it, it was pretty clear – it had actually been penned by the Prince himself. This was a statement that came straight from the heart – so much so that some people wondered if Harry's older brother William would be concerned at both the tone and the content, not least as the relationship was at that point still a new one, and he perhaps felt Harry might have been wiser to remain tight-lipped about it until it had run a little bit longer. In the event, however, it emerged that William, who was very close to his brother, supported the move. The statement also made it quite clear that Harry had fallen head over heels. But it was also a sign that the relationship was far more serious than anyone had realised.

Speculation had been mounting for weeks that

romance was in the air: although the two had not actually been pictured together, the beautiful American actress Meghan Markle was increasingly believed to be Harry's new girlfriend and it was the fact that some people were delving into her life and trying to find out more about her that had prompted the blast from the Palace. Harry clearly did not want history to repeat itself. The Prince had had two significant relationships in the past with Chelsy Davy and Cressida Bonas, but by the middle of 2016 had been single for a couple of years, although he often spoke movingly of his longing to settle down and start a family, like William. The relationship with Meghan could prove the happy ending the entire country was so keen for Harry to have, and for all his natural concern about his new girlfriend the intense interest in Meghan was also a sign of how much the nation held Harry to its collective heart.

For now it seemed that the woman with whom he might find his happy ending had finally appeared. The hints were there and mounting: sharp-eyed observers had spotted that the two of them had been pictured separately wearing the same blue-and-white bracelet, surely more than just a coincidence. Harry was wearing his when he attended a rehearsal of The Joyful Noise Choir, which was made up of people living with HIV, and which prompted more comments about how well suited the two of them were because they were both interested in good causes.

Indeed, they were said to have met in early 2016 when Harry visited Toronto on behalf of the Invictus Games, which he had founded in 2014 as a Paralympic-style sports event featuring wounded, injured or sick armed forces personnel, and which had been a huge success.

Meghan, meanwhile, had tweeted a picture of two bananas spooning after rumours of the relationship had surfaced, which if not exactly a confirmation, certainly seemed to betoken a happy state of mind. More details began to surface: Meghan had even been seen in the Royal Box at Wimbledon on 28 June and 4 July. She was, still though, relatively unknown in the UK. Meghan played paralegal Rachel Zane in US legal drama *Suits*, it emerged, and the tabloids were overjoyed when they found that not only had she recently filmed 'steamy scenes' with co-star Mike Ross, but that she was a divorcee, after a brief marriage a couple of years previously. She is thought to have met and got on with William and Kate, crucial for any successful relationship with Harry, for he is extremely close to his brother and sister-in-law.

Meanwhile, Kensington Palace refused to comment. Coral stopped taking bets on the likelihood of a Royal engagement in 2017; Buckingham Palace said it wouldn't comment on Harry's private life. It was also reported that Meghan was still seeing her previous boyfriend when she met Harry and that after he'd 'bombarded' her with texts she'd finally agreed to give it a whirl; various newspaper columnists began to opine that she was just what the Royal family needed. Newspapers which had totally ignored *Suits* until then begun to run reviews. In truth, before the story broke on 31 October 2016, the vast majority of Britons would have struggled to identify Meghan; within twenty-four hours she'd become a household name.

Once unleashed, the frenzy showed no sign of dying down. Meghan's half-sister was sought out for (none too complimentary) comment. Meghan was reported to have met Prince Charles. Harry was said to have cancelled a trip to Toronto, seemingly unwilling to add fuel to the flames, but there was no dampening down public interest now. It was counterclaimed that he had done no such thing and had made it to Meghan's Toronto home for Hallowe'en. A summer trip made by the two of them to Balmoral came to light. Some more troubling comments emerged: it turned out that Meghan was mixed race, with a black mother, and in the more unsavoury quarters of social media some unpleasant comment was made. Worse, if anything, was that clips from *Suits* surfaced on the repulsive Pornhub site. They almost certainly wouldn't have made it there had it not been revealed that Meghan was dating a Windsor, and there were clearly those who were all too happy to try and make trouble for Harry and his new girl. And some of it sparkled with a touch of the ridiculous: an ex-Royal butler was wheeled out to say that as an ex-model, Meghan would have elegant posture at formal dinners, which was sure to go down well with the rest of the clan.

Still neither seemed in any hurry to confirm or deny anything, however, until speculation in some quarters reached such a level of prurience that something within Harry seemed to snap. He reached for his communications secretary and issued the statement which, somewhat ironically, was the first public confirmation that the two were indeed a pair. Nor did it do anything to lessen the interest in the two of them. But it did make it clear that this was a serious love affair. Public affection for Harry had never been higher and there was a palpable hope in the air that at long last Charles and Diana's younger son, who had lost his mother when he was just twelve years old, had finally found the woman with whom he could share his life. For while with the birth of his nephew, Prince George, and niece, Princess Charlotte, he had dropped to the position of fifth in line to the throne, Prince Harry still had all the burdens of an active Royal life and no one with whom to share them. And although it had at that point been nineteen years since Diana, Princess of Wales had been tragically killed in a car accident in a Paris underpass, there was still something of the Little Boy Lost about Harry. He might have been a man in his thirties with a military career behind him, but to many he was still the little boy who had emerged into the public spotlight, blinking and clinging on to the hand of his father, to view the sea of flowers that covered London in the wake of the death of his mother. Only marriage and a family of his own would ever really erase that.

Both Harry's earlier girlfriends, Chelsy and Cressida had been unable to cope with the attention that accompanied a relationship with the world's most eligible bachelor, with the result in both cases that the romances came to an end. That was clearly in Harry's mind when he released his statement: concern that the spotlight might drive Meghan away. He had also spoken in the past about the difficulties of forming a relationship with anyone, for the simple reason that even if he was spotted so much as talking to a woman, she was immediately labelled a girlfriend-cum-potential wife, which put an intolerable pressure on everyone involved, especially the woman, and made it very difficult for an actual relationship to start.

During interviews with the BBC and *The Sunday*

Times in May 2016 (around the time he'd met Meghan, although no one knew it at the time) while opening the Invictus Games, Harry had talked about the problems of starting a new relationship. 'Even if I talk to a girl, that person is then suddenly my wife, and people go knocking on her door,' he said. 'Everyone has a right to their privacy, and a lot of the members of the public get it, but sadly in some areas there is this incessant need to find out every little bit of detail about what goes on behind the scene. It's unnecessary. If or when I do find a girlfriend, I will do my utmost to ensure that me and her can get to the point where we're actually comfortable with each other before the massive invasion that is inevitably going to happen into her privacy.' Was he thinking of Meghan even then? Probably so.

But Meghan was very different from the women he had so far been serious about. For a start, although until then Harry had seemed to favour blondes, Meghan was a very striking brunette – with, as many were not slow to point out, an uncanny resemblance to Harry's sister-in law, Pippa Middleton, with whom he had frequently been seen enjoying time with in the past. Secondly, and more to the point, she was far more of a woman of the world than her two predecessors, who were both extremely young when they dated their Prince and had never had a chance to develop out of the public eye. Three years older than Harry, at thirty-five, she had already been divorced – bringing into sharp focus the way the monarchy had changed over the previous century. Divorce had been the topic that had haunted the Windsor's throughout the twentieth century, causing at least one crisis that rocked the monarchy to its foundations and untold heartbreak for others along the way.

Indeed, the reason that Harry's grandmother was the UK's monarch was directly related to a divorcee. Less than a hundred years earlier Harry's Great-Great-Uncle Edward had abdicated the throne because of his love for an American, the twice-wed Wallis Simpson, and while the two of them did then get married, Edward went on to lead what many saw as a sad and empty existence. He paid a very high price for finding love in the wrong place and he and his wife were never entirely forgiven for having, shockingly to many, placed personal happiness above Edward's duty to his country. Queen Elizabeth the Queen Mother, in particular, blamed the two of them for the pressures piled on Edward's younger brother Albert, her husband, who went on to become King George VI.

Of course, Harry was not King when he fell for Meghan, nestling a full five steps away from the throne at the time and further still at the time of writing, and attitudes towards divorce had changed seismically, both among the Royal family and the public, but even so, American ladies had caused problems for princes of the realm in the past. Nor was that all: there had been more recent and unhappy precedents as well. Harry's Great-Aunt Margaret had also fallen for an older divorcee, in her case her father's equerry, the dashing Captain Peter Townsend. He had proposed and Margaret clearly wanted to marry him, but in the stiff moral climate of the 1950s had been forced to make a choice between love and Royal duty. She chose the latter and while this was the opposite of what Edward had been deemed to have done, she too went on to lead a sadly unfulfilled life, ironically getting divorced herself from the man she did eventually marry, Antony Armstrong-Jones, the Earl of Snowdon. An aura of sadness seemed to surround her, no matter that she led a hedonistic life. It was, on the surface, unfair: Edward chose love over duty and suffered; Margaret did the opposite and also suffered. Ultimately, it emerged that one of the reasons Margaret did not follow her heart was that she had not wanted to give up the status that being a member of the Royal family entailed, which put a slightly different complexion on matters, but even so, she had been put in a remarkably difficult position, probably unnecessarily, and she had paid a very high price.

Harry's Uncle Andrew had had a similar experience which also didn't have the fairy-tale ending that is supposed to lie in wait for a prince. In his youth, while, like Harry, a dashing member of the military forces, he had become involved with another American actress, Koo Stark, in this case not a divorcee but with a past that was still deemed too racy for the times. The two had been an item for a year and a half before the news became public, at which point Andrew too was forced to give her up. He might just have managed to get away with having an American significant other – still an issue in the early 1980s – but Koo had unfortunately once appeared in a saucy film and that was enough to rule her out. By today's standards the film was so tame as to be almost risible – but at that stage the public and, more to the point, the advisors to the Royal family, simply would not have countenanced even this mild misdemeanour. History seemed to be repeating itself. Again it had ended unhappily for everyone involved. Koo never married; her subsequent relationship with the father of her child ended in extremely acrimonious circumstances and she encountered any number of personal misfortunes. Andrew, of course, did marry, but while his relationship with the former Sarah Ferguson was to remain a good one, the couple did divorce amid much controversy.

Again there was a case of a Windsor seeming to do his duty and being forced to suffer for it. However, things were beginning to change. Harry knew all that. He also knew that just a generation previously such a relationship as the one he was having with Meghan would have been absolutely impossible. But then he had yet another very different unhappy example to learn from as well: the disastrous relationship of his parents. For a start, Prince Charles would not have been allowed to marry the woman he really wanted (and eventually did marry), the young Camilla Shand, who was not (yet) married and divorced. She, of course, went on to marry Andrew Parker Bowles. Prince Charles was forced to look elsewhere. Lady Diana Spencer, from an old aristocratic family that had served as courtiers to the Royals for centuries, had seemed a perfect choice for the Prince, then in his early thirties (the same age as Harry, in fact, when he met Meghan), when he came under serious pressure to wed. Young, pretty and apparently malleable, she looked certain to be able to give Charles the stable domestic backdrop that he needed in his role as second most important Royal after the Queen, to say nothing of providing him with an heir. To all but a very small number in the Royal family, the match appeared a fairy tale in the making. The then Archbishop of Canterbury,

Dr Robert Runcie, who presided over the proceedings, said the marriage was 'the stuff of fairy tales'.

In fact, of course, the opposite was the case. The two proved to be totally unsuited temperamentally and the world watched in horror as the marriage painfully, loudly and publicly fell apart. Princes William and Harry were brought up in a marital war zone and as both parents sought to gain the upper hand over the other, the War of the Waleses became a staple of newspaper features, to say nothing of the books published. Any child whose parents' divorce goes through a traumatic experience, but in this case it was in the full glare of the public spotlight, with the two little boys at the centre of it all forced to endure not just the split but the fact that everyone in the world, it seemed, knew all about the trauma. Even worse, they (and the world) became acquainted with the minutiae of their parents' love lives as each blamed the other for straying from the marital bonds; it was an almost unendurable torment for a child, which then proceeded to get even worse. After the couple's divorce, William and Harry might have been expected to find some peace from all the acrimony, but instead, just over a year later, Diana was dead, killed in a car accident in a Parisian underpass. Harry was twelve at the time. It gave both the young Princes a profound mistrust of the press:

whatever the truth about what happened that night, the car in which Diana and her boyfriend, Dodi Fayed, were being driven was being chased by a pack of paparazzi on motorbikes. Paparazzi are actually quite different from most journalists, and indeed press photographers, but it was not a distinction that two grieving sons could be expected to draw. From then on the two of them were very wary about possible press intrusion, something that would have been uppermost in Harry's mind when he released his statement to the press.

The tragedy of their mother's death alone would have been enough to leave them scarred for life, but on top of it all was the fact that three of Elizabeth II's four children ended up in the divorce courts, as did her sister. Her own marriage to Prince Philip was a rock-solid one, but the two had been unable to pass on to their children the art of staying married – and that only a few decades after the divorce-related Abdication crisis, which had rocked the monarchy to its very foundations. It was an irony not lost on anyone and it was one of the reasons that the younger Royals were being permitted to live their lives in a very different way from the past. Harry's older brother William had been allowed to live with his girlfriend Kate Middleton before the two of them married, and while that would have been unthinkable to an earlier generation, it had resulted in one of the most successful Royal relationships in years.

Kate, of course, was also not the sort of person who would once have been considered marriage material for a future king: not only were her parents middle-class business people but her mother comes from north-eastern coal-mining stock. But the lessons of the past had been learned: better that a Windsor be allowed to marry for love rather than be paired off with someone whose parents were deemed appropriate. And in her case she was at least British and with no serious prior romantic entanglements to speak of. A very few eyebrows might have been raised at the marriage among the more traditional in the Royal circles, but the overwhelming feeling was one of relief that a senior Windsor had at last got his choice of significant other right.

A similar leniency was being extended to Harry. Chelsy Davy had not been without baggage, and she came across as a fun-loving party girl, albeit one who didn't put a foot wrong and was clearly very attached to Harry. There would have been no barriers placed in their path had they decided to wed. Cressida Bonas, meanwhile, came from a bohemian aristocratic background in which both parents were much-married, and also worked as an actress. Again, no obstacles were set in that path.

And so the appearance of Meghan Markle, and the fact that she was accepted by everyone from the outset, marked a seismic change not just in the Royal family, but in everyone else as well. People wanted Harry to have his happy ending: it was not just the tragedy of his childhood that marked out a special place for him in the public's feelings, but the fact that despite the odd gaffe he was clearly, in the language of the vernacular, a seriously good bloke. Since leaving the Army he had been making valuable contributions to society, especially with the Invictus Games, and like his mother, had the common touch. William could sometimes appear stiff and uneasy; not so his younger brother, who was relaxed, chatty and able to get on with anyone, from any background, anywhere, anytime. And now, it seems, he has found his future princess. So just who is Meghan Markle – or Princess Meghan, as she would now be known?

CHAPTER 2

A STAR IN THE MAKING

The 1970s was a time of huge cultural change in the United States. It encompassed Watergate, the end of the Vietnam War and the election of President Reagan. The wider world was altering beyond all recognition, too. It was a decade that witnessed the rise of feminism, the oil crisis, the death of Mao Zedong, the election of Margaret Thatcher as Britain's first female prime minister, the Egyptian–Israel Peace Treaty and the Iranian Revolution. In the UK, there were mutterings about something else too. Prince Charles was by the end of the decade in his thirties, and the next in line to the British throne was expected to marry and himself produce an heir. In a scenario his sons would come to recognise, every time he was pictured with a new woman, she was spoken of as a potential bride. But who would finally capture the Prince's heart?

Back in the Republican US of A, those were minor considerations, if indeed anyone was aware of them at all. Quite apart from all the other seismic changes taking place across society, it was also the decade in which the Civil Rights Movement of the 1960s began to filter through into everyday life: the United States was still torn apart by race issues, but for the first time, African Americans were being accorded equal rights and opportunities (in theory, at least) with their white counterparts. It was a time of massive social upheaval that affected everyone, and which was going to have a direct impact on Meghan Markle and her own family.

But real change happens slowly, and in a country with the tortured history of race relations of the United States, where slavery casts such a long and dark shadow to this day, just about no person of colour is untouched by the issue. Michelle Obama, the first African-American First Lady, is a case in point: even her ancestors were victims of the slave trade. Meghan was to grow up aware of those tensions. The mixed-race element of her background was also the source of much comment when she finally met her prince.

For although attitudes had begun to change in some of the big cities, across a great deal of the United States, there was still a huge amount of prejudice against mixed-race relationships, prejudice that would be directed at Harry and Meghan, Meghan's parents and even couples further back in her family history. That racial element was another of the reasons for Harry's explosion in anger – and surely the release of the press statement – while Meghan took it in good heart, one of the reasons being surely, apart from an innate good nature, that she grew up with it. Harry, the product of a 1,000-year-old monarchy, would never have come across prejudice of any kind (apart from the odd republican); above all, not one directed at the colour of his skin.

In the US, however, it was an issue. It was towards the end of that decade of change, the 1970s, that Doria Ragland, a yoga therapist and social worker, and Thomas W. Markle, a director of photography, first met. And when the news of their daughter's romance with Prince Harry first broke, it took a little while for the penny to drop with excited onlookers and, more pertinently, a media obsessed with the potential new princess, that Meghan Markle was not one of the pretty blonde types that Harry had been associated with in the past. But when it did, it was the reporting on her parentage and the term 'exotic' that caused particular offence, for Meghan is the offspring of a mixed-race couple. Her mother is African American and her father is Caucasian. It was an issue for Meghan herself: aware that she was the product of two different ethnic backgrounds, she has spoken of being torn between them – and that without the attention that comes from being in a relationship with a prince.

And while her background should not have raised the eyebrows it did, nor indeed cause the slightly barbed remarks that filtered her way, again, it cannot be emphasised enough that the United States is still torn apart by the racial divide that Meghan has been aware of all her life. And although the United Kingdom isn't to the same degree, racial tensions still exist, even though the situation has improved massively in recent decades. But mixed-race relationships throughout society do still cause comment, and while Britain may not have quite the issues with race that the US does, it is exceedingly class conscious, for all the changes that have taken place in society. Families remain proud of their titles and their heritage – *too* proud in some cases – and newcomers marrying into the family can still be subject to a great deal of scrutiny.

There was a recent precedent for Harry to dwell on: when Ceawlin Thynn, aka Viscount Weymouth and the heir to the Marquess of Bath, married Emma McQuiston in 2013, his mother is said to have made the deeply unpleasant remark, 'Are you sure about what you're doing to 400 years of bloodline?' Like Meghan, Emma is of mixed parentage: her mother, Suzanna McQuiston, (who described Lady Bath as 'racist' and 'ghastly') is white and her father, Ladi Jadesimi, is a Nigerian oil tycoon. (Lady Bath, who is actually Hungarian, point-blank denied being racist or using the language ascribed to her.) That said, most of the coverage when the wedding took place was positive, with much talk of Britain's first black marchioness, photoshoots in *Tatler* and magazines like *Hello!*, and cheerful comment. The country was clearly ready for a black princess as well as a black marchioness, or a mixed-race one, or whatever anyone wished to call her.

In fact, Meghan's parentage is slightly more complicated than it has often been portrayed because it is not a simple case of one white parent and one black parent: it seems almost certain that there were a number of other mixed-race marriages in her background generations before her parents first got together. And again, in class-conscious Britain, these things are at the very least a point of interest nowadays, if not the cause of the outright snobbery they would once have been. And Harry is not the only one with documented heritage: Doria's roots have been traced as far back as 1881 when Meghan's great-great grandfather, Jeremiah (Jerry) Ragland, was born in Clayton, Georgia: his mother, who was white, was called Texas 'Texie' Hendrick, while his father, Steve Ragland, was probably black. A newspaper commissioned a genealogist to discover that Jeremiah was described in the 1920 census as 'mulatto' – someone born to black and white parents, something massively more unusual and unconventional then than would be the case today and also a term that would never be used nearly 100 years down the line.

Jeremiah went on to marry Claudie Ritchie, and the couple moved to Chattanooga, a pleasant and in places elegant city nestling in the foothills of the Appalachian Mountains in Tennessee. Jeremiah had some success in life in that he owned his own tailoring shop, while Claudie worked as a maid at Miller's Department Store, in which black and white staff were kept separate and white customers were served by the latter only. At that point, segregation existed in every aspect of life across the United States and Miller's clientele clearly extended only to the fair-skinned element in the town.

'Miller Brothers carried the finest fashions and home décor, and sponsored events in keeping with their image,' said the local newspaper, *The Chattanoogan*. 'In 1967, they hosted a "Hail, Britannia" collection, which included replicas of English jewelry and china. Representatives from Great Britain attended the gala. Miller Brothers was already known for its tea room, so the Britannia event was natural.'

Of course, this was some time after Claudie's stint there: she died at the age of forty-four, while Jeremiah lived to sixty-three. Life in a mixed-race family at the end of the nineteenth century and beginning of the twentieth would have been extremely difficult at a time when racism was essentially enshrined in US law, and it is a sad indictment on US society that tensions over just such a family grouping were still there when Meghan was born over 100 years on.

But from 1877 to 1965, the year civil-rights legislation was enacted, the 'Jim Crow' laws ensured that blacks were treated like second-class citizens: they were forced to use totally different (and markedly inferior) facilities to whites, the two different colours didn't eat together, they lived in separate areas and attended separate schools, rode either on separate trains or in different parts of the same train, and so it went on. Blacks could not stay in the same hotels as whites, eat in the same restaurants, or have anything like the same opportunities accorded to whites in the 'land of the free'.

The wider world became more aware of this at the start of the Civil Rights Movement when Rosa Parks refused to give up her seat on a bus to a white person as she was legally obliged to do, and kicked off the huge protests that would eventually lead to changes in the law. But shocking as this was, bus segregation was nothing compared to the other privations the black community was forced to endure.

Be all that as it may, such couplings clearly took place, with Meghan's family as elsewhere, and the family grew. The couple, Jerry and Claudie, lived with their son, Steve, daughters, Dora, a teacher, and Lillie, a cook, and the latter's husband, Robert Calloway, a janitor. Steve, Meghan's great-grandfather, was born *c.* 1908 and died in 1983. Steve married Lois Russell in 1929, and worked as a presser in a cleaning shop. The couple had a son called Alvin, Meghan's grandfather, who died aged eighty-one in 2011 and who was married to Ava Burrow. She worked for Hamilton County Schools, and the couple then moved to Cailifornia, where Meghan's mother, Doria, was born.

The Jim Crow laws might have been repealed, but such entrenched racism and appalling discrimination against people of colour could not disappear overnight and as the 1992 race riots in Los Angeles prove, there is still a very long way to go before the different races can live in accord, side by side. By Meghan's own account, in an unflinchingly honest article in *Elle* magazine about growing up mixed race, her parents met towards the end of the 1970s when her father Thomas, of Dutch-Irish descent and originally from Pennsylviania, was working as a lighting director for a soap opera and her mother was temping on set. Thomas already had two children from a previous relationship, Samantha and Thomas Jr, who were to cause headlines of their own when news of their younger half-sister's relationship came out.

The pair married and moved to The Valley in Los Angeles, a leafy and comfortable area that was also predominantly white. Doria, 'caramel in complexion', according to her daughter, was often assumed to be Meghan's nanny rather than her mother, on the grounds that with a white father, Meghan had lighter skin. By her own account, Meghan's parents worked as hard as they could to prevent her from becoming aware of any racial tensions when she was still young, at one point buying two collections of a boxed set of Barbie dolls that she'd expressed a wish for, one portraying a white family and the other a black one. They then mixed the two up to show a black mother, white father and one each of the children, and presented it as just the one set. There were, it seems, no sets of dolls to be bought that portrayed a mixed-race family at the time.

But with all the goodwill in the world, Doria and Thomas were never going to be able to shield their daughter forever from what was going on in the rest of the world. These days, people are required to fill out forms that give multiple options not only for race but for gender; it was different back then. Meghan recalled her feelings of confusion at the age of seven when asked to tick a box confirming her ethnicity: there was nothing for mixed-race children and so, rather than having to choose one parent's identity over the other – black or white – she left it blank, despite a teacher advising her to choose the white option on the grounds she had light skin. When she told her father what had happened he was unequivocal: 'If that happens again, you draw your own box.' Thomas was enraged on his daughter's behalf and continued to try to protect her from hurt, much of it unthinking, as she grew up.

By that time, alas, the marriage was over, which in the years to come meant that Meghan and Harry would both know what it was like to come from a broken family. Her mother and father split when Meghan was just six although she maintained a very good relationship with both parents. Meghan continued to live with her mother, and in so doing developed a big sense of adventure, travelling the world from a young age (a little like Harry, in fact) when her mother was working as a travel agent and seeing a great deal more than her contemporaries. She remembered this in a newspaper interview.

'I got the travel bug quite early,' she told the *Chicago Tribune*. 'My earliest memories are of going to Mexico twice a year and Hawaii quite a few times. We never did conventional family trips like Disney World. Hawaii and Mexico were closer for us than going to Florida or the Caribbean. You know, this is all I knew. Just like being an only child was all I knew. I was always aware of how unique and cool it was that my mom got to take me to all these cool places because of her job and connections.'

Meghan, though, clearly didn't feel she'd missed out: 'It was so much fun traveling, primarily with my mom. I never felt envious of the more cookie cutter-type of vacations, although I'm sure those would have been wonderful, too. But my mom never wanted me to just go to a resort and not leave the property, and think that was all there was to visiting a foreign country. We liked going to Oaxaca, Mexico, and tried to really get an authentic cultural experience.'

Her mother was also a yoga afficionado and would practice with her daughter, who would go on to become very interested in yoga as an adult. And while Meghan was an only child of her two biological parents, she did have two older half-siblings and she got on very well with at least one of them. Thomas, fourteen years her senior, had children of his own by the time Meghan entered her teens: 'She used to like to take us to the dark park,' her nephew Tyler, Thomas's son recalled. 'We would feed the ducks and run to the park when she babysat [me and my brother Thomas].'

Meghan displayed a quite preternatural sense of confidence, which was displayed in an episode when she was still only eleven. She was offended by an advertisement by a soap manufacturer that she felt implied women belonged in the kitchen so she wrote to the then First Lady Hillary Clinton, among other prominent women, to complain. This early stab at campaigning – she was to do a lot more in later life – worked and the advertisement was changed. Meghan was in later years to have a profile that she could put to good use, but in this particular case all she had was determination. She was to learn that would work as well.

She was certainly a feisty little girl and her campaigning spirit surfaced early. 'I was eleven or twelve years old when I became a member of the National Organization for Women in the States,' she told Matchesfashion.com. 'I've always been a young feminist, and looking back, I guess there are all kinds of pieces to that puzzle. It's always been important to me to be vocal about what I feel is right, whether that's as a woman, or being bi-racial. I think so much of it is when you can't find which box you can tick, or where you fit in. My dad always taught me to just make your own box, so that's always been part of how I moved in the world since I was young. An outspoken little one – oh, my goodness, a handful! But I think it's just who I am.'

Her propensity towards activism was also affected by the 1992 riots in Los Angeles, which went on for six days and which claimed 55 lives, injured over 2,000 people and resulted in numerous cases of arson, looting and assault. The riots were sparked after four police officers were cleared of using excessive violence in the arrest of Rodney King: there had been footage of the arrest, however, showing police beating King as he lay on the ground following a high-speed car chase. There was of course a racial element to it: King was black and the officers were white. Meghan was witnessing at close hand one of the most notorious racial injustices in her own home city.

These early experiences were to play a huge role in later life when, alongside her career as an actress, she also became something of a social campaigner. She started young. 'I started working at a soup kitchen in skid row of Los Angeles when I was thirteen years old, and the first day I felt really scared,' she was reported as saying in *The Game Changers*, a book by Samantha Brett and Steph Adams.

'I was young, and it was rough and raw down there, and though I was with a great volunteer group, I just felt overwhelmed. I remember one of my mentors (Mrs Maria Pollia) told me that "life is about putting others' needs above your own fears". That has always stayed with me. Yes, make sure you are safe and never ever put yourself in a compromising situation, but once that is checked off the list, I think it's really important for us to remember that someone needs us, and that your act of giving/helping/doing can truly become an act of grace once you get out of your head.'

Meghan remained close to her father, who by now was working on one of the most popular television shows in the United States, a sitcom called *Married... with Children,* and in so doing proved to be quite as definitive an influence on his daughter's future and the nature of her character as her mother. Meghan spent a lot of time with him on set, becoming familiar with the set-up of a television show from a very young age, and getting used to being around actors, directors and the whole crowd involved in the medium. This early grounding in the world of acting clearly left its mark – it was a world that was to become second nature to her when she was still very young and it is hardly surprising that it is where she went on to make her career.

Meghan acknowledged as much. 'My dad was a lighting director and director of photography,' she told *Esquire* in 2013. 'He just retired actually last year. Every day after school for ten years, I was on the set of *Married... with Children*, which is a really funny and perverse place for a little girl in a Catholic school uniform to grow up. There were a lot of times my dad would say, "Meg, why don't you go and help with the craft services room over there? This is just a little off-colour for your eleven-year-old eyes." Yeah. I wasn't allowed to watch it at home.'

But she was allowed a charming little gesture by her mother. 'I could watch the end credits so I could give the screen a kiss when I saw my dad's name go by,' Meghan said. 'You gotta think, there were guest stars like Tia Carrere and Traci Lords and Nikki Cox. Those were the kind of women coming in every day. Just picture me with my curly hair and a gap in my teeth and my little school uniform with Keds on, looking up like, "Hi," at these very, uh, provocative women. It was a big change from

Immaculate Heart Catholic School.' She was, however, a very pretty child, already clearly a beauty in the making.

Life on set taught Meghan a lot about life and not just about acting and lighting. For a start, it turned her into a foodie, surrounded as she was by the crew's catering, which was something else that was to become an obsession in later years. 'That's where I started to learn about garnishing and plating,' she told *Best Health* magazine. 'After being there every day after school for ten years and seeing the appreciation of food, I started to learn the association between food and happiness and being able to entertain – I think that's where the seed was planted.'

It also taught her some of the tricks of her own future profession, especially where lighting was involved. 'I will always find my light. No question,' she told *Esquire*. 'And if I don't, I'll know, because my dad will be the first person to call me and say like, "You need to have him bring another 2K in," and "Why aren't you using this sort of lighting gel?" The crew guys know that it's where I grew up.'

But while Meghan was learning her trade on set, there was still the more conventional education to undergo. As she referred to earlier, she attended the Immaculate Heart Catholic High School, which was an all-girl,

Catholic school also referred to as the Immaculate Heart Convent, and it has been the alma mater of more than a few big Hollywood stars. Lucie Arnaz attended, as did Tyra Banks, Mary Tyler Moore and Ione Skye. And one Immaculate Heart woman looked like she might be becoming a princess...

One word that is used a lot in conjunction with Meghan is 'classy' and she was showing that quality right from the start. While not a swot *per se*, she was determined to succeed at school and put her head down and got on with it. 'Meghan was really charismatic and was a very hard worker and very focused and you could tell she was going to do something special with her life,' said one school friend.

She also picked up some talents that would stand her in good stead in later years at a time when she was breaking into acting but had to support herself with other jobs on the side. Many actresses wait on tables, but Meghan discovered her quite beautiful handwriting was an even better way to help her earn her daily bread, a skill she was taught when she was still very young.

'It was because I went to an all-girls Catholic school for like six years during the time when kids actually had handwriting class,' she told *Esquire*. 'I've always had a propensity for getting the cursive down pretty well. What it evolved into was my pseudo-waitressing job when I was auditioning. I didn't wait tables. I did calligraphy for the invitations for, like, Robin Thicke and Paula Patton's wedding. I used to do it for Dolce & Gabbana's celebrity correspondence over the holidays. I would sit there with a little white tube sock on my hand so no hand oils got on the card, trying to pay my bills while auditioning. I'm glad that in the land of no one seeming to appreciate a handwritten note anymore that I can try to keep that alive.'

After news of Meghan's relationship with Harry emerged, photographs surfaced of Meghan at school. They show a remarkably self-possessed looking young woman, beaming and athletic, in some of the shots looking over her shoulder, ready to take on the world. Bright, optimistic and confident, even in those early pictures it was clear that Meghan would be making something of herself in later life.

She was girl scout too, with her mother being the leader of her troop, and started taking an interest in acting while still at school, taking part in projects including musical comedy *Damn Yankees!*, with the nearby all-boys school, Loyola. 'Meghan acted as a [teaching assistant] in drama and most kids our age wouldn't have felt as confident in their skills. She was bubbly, optimistic and positive. She was also very focused and had her eye on the prize – she knew where she wanted to go to college and she knew she wanted to do drama. She had the talent and focus to back it up and you could tell she knew the work it would take and she was willing to put in the work', said a classmate. Meghan did not reach the dizzy heights of prom queen when she was at high school, but it is thought she was homecoming queen, the person nominated to represent the school at homecoming (school reunion) events.

It was all a way of turning her into a remarkably self-possessed young woman. Travels with her mother were also a further way of adding to her extra-curricular education and building up that confidence. It was at the root of interests she developed later in life, too – both parents had an active role in making her the person she would become and, crucially, provided a childhood that would enable her to mix with people from all walks of life.

'[Travel] really shapes you from a young age and makes you really empathetic of people of whatever culture, wherever they're from,' she told *Esquire*. 'It made me much more courageous to take myself out of a sheltered bubble... Growing up in Hollywood, I was around the entertainment industry all the time. I knew I'd end up in showbusiness in some capacity, eventually. But when I was young, I knew I wanted to try something else. So it was wonderful to be in the foreign services and live in Buenos Aires [which she did as a young adult]. I think that kind of life experience can only help in your performance as an actor.'

And so it did. But before she was ready to start her career, Meghan was off to university, the first member of her family to do so. Yet more barriers were falling down.

CHAPTER 3

DIPLOMATIC RELATIONS

Meghan got the drama bug at school and it grew while she was at university, but, in an intriguing aside, it looked briefly as if she might become a diplomat instead – in which case, of course, there would have been every chance of meeting Harry on the international circuit. Whether romance would have blossomed is another matter. But first there was the matter of further education to consider: after leaving school Meghan attended Northwestern University, a very well-respected academic institution based in the Chicago suburb of Evanston, Illinois.

It was very different from the temperate Californian climate: temperatures plummeted to freezing in the winter, while the boiling hot summers were also very humid, something Meghan sometimes found difficult to cope with. She worked as hard there as she had done at school, and still dabbled in amateur acting, as well as studying it – in fact, her degree hinted that a career in the US Department of State, the equivalent of the UK's Foreign Office, was seriously on the cards. It also illustrated that she was interested in campaigning work. That said, she had an eye towards acting from very early on – 'I remember going to class at Northwestern, sitting there and wondering if I could make it. I had a commercial agent in Chicago and I would drive into the city and try to build this career,' she once said.

Meghan graduated in 2003 with a double major in theatre and international relations (which meant that both were considered to be the subject she took her degree in, indicating some ambivalence about her future path). She was, in her own words, the 'theatre nerd', active and interested even then. Once she started to make a name for herself in TV series *Suits*, she paid a return visit to her alma mater: 'It's surreal being back because I haven't been back since I graduated and as I am walking around I remember things like the schlep of getting to South Campus from up north,' she told the university newspaper *North by Northwestern*. 'The

24-hour Burger King also definitely helped me put on the Freshman Fifteen.'

It was in fact while still at university that she got the first in a series of opportunities that would send her on her way; she met someone who, post-graduation, would help her with a very useful introduction. 'I had gone home for the holidays and a friend from college had invited me to a party,' she told the *South China Morning Post*. 'There was a manager there. My friend gave him a student film I had made with her and he called me and said: "You're going to make money and I want to take 10 per cent." It was very lucky, come to think of it, just to have someone give you a break so easily. It was like getting discovered at Schwab's [a popular hangout for movie actors and industry dealmakers, where Hollywood legend has it, Lana Turner was discovered].'

Meghan was going to have to pay her dues, however. 'But that doesn't mean it was always easy,' she continued. 'No matter what gets your foot in the door, you have to be able to get all of you in the door. At one of my first auditions, I just had this moxy; maybe it came from working at the Embassy [of which more anon], but I had confidence. I had gone in for a film and the part was Girl No.1 and the line was: "Hi." That was it. The director and the casting people were there, and he said: "Can you say, 'Hi'?" And I said, "I can. However, I've read the script and I really respond to this other role and I'd like to audition for that." This panic spread across the room because who does that? Who takes that sort of risk?'

However, Meghan did not embark on a career in acting as soon as she left Northwestern. That taste for both travel and campaigning led her in a very different direction altogether at first, before she realised that the entertainment industry was where she wanted to be. 'I had always been the theatre nerd at Northwestern University,' she told *Marie Claire*. 'I knew I wanted to do acting, but I hated the idea of being this cliché – a girl from LA who decides to be an actress. I wanted more than that, and I had always loved politics, so I ended up changing my major completely, and double-majoring in theatre and international relations. By my junior year I had finished most of my credits, and so I applied for an internship at the US Embassy... I ended up working in the Embassy in Buenos Aires for a few months. It was their economic devaluation and our Secretary of the Treasury at the time, Paul O'Neill, was there, so I'm twenty years old, in Buenos Aires, in a motorcade, doing that whole thing. I thought for sure I would still have a career in politics.' That rather adventurous outing was followed by a period in Madrid.

However, it was when Meghan returned that she went to *that* party and met her potential manager which, she later admitted, lulled her into a false sense of security about the career she was to choose. 'I was really spoilt because I booked my first audition, so it's the biggest tease because you think, "Oh, this is easy",' she said in her *Suits* days. 'All things considered, I'm so grateful and fortunate that I have a show now that's doing well, but it's not easy. It was definitely a struggle.'

Indeed, Meghan might have made good contacts while she was still at college but her career started gently at first. Her first documented role was in 2002 as Jill in one episode of the long-running American soap opera *General Hospital*, set in the large upstate New York city of Port Charles, which has been running since 1963. From there it was back to the calligraphy as Meghan's next reported role was as Natasha in *Century City*, a full two years later.

This could be seen as a forerunner for the series, *Suits*, which brought her to the wider public as it also centred on a legal practice, but it was a very different kettle of fish. For a start it was set in the future, 2030, based on the legal team of Crane, Constable, McNeil & Montero, and the characters were given all sorts of complex future ethical dilemmas to worry about, such as cloning cells, genetic profiling and mind-altering antibiotics. Secondly, it was an absolute dud. CBS ordered nine episodes, but in the event aired only four of them, including Meghan's, titled 'A Mind Is A Terrible Thing To Lose': it was originally intended to be the eighth episode and actually was shown as the fourth.

However, in the event, the remaining five episodes were picked up and screened by Universal HD and they are still available to see on Hulu.com. Really, the only memorable episode in Meghan's life that year (2004) was when she met her future husband, film producer Trevor Engelson. Born on 23 October 1976, Engelson comes from Great Neck, New York, and was educated first at Great Neck North and then at the prestigious Annenberg School for Communication at the University of California, and, on paper at least, the pair seemed very compatible. Engelson was another who worked in the film industry: he started off as a production assistant on *Deep Blue Sea*, which starred Samuel L. Jackson and LL Cool J, and from there moved on to the Endeavour Talent Agency, becoming an agent.

Engelson is clearly an earthy individual and a free spirit, much like his wife-to-be. He decided that Endeavour was not for him, on the grounds that it was too corporate, and decided to branch out on his own. But the parting was amicable: 'They were nice to me – they said, "We like you, but you're not going to be an agent here. But you can stay as long as you can until you find a job.'"

Engelson went on to become one of the so-called 'Young Turks' of Hollywood, a member of the younger generation taking on the older crowd. He started his own company, Underground, with his then partner Nick Osborne and moved into management and production. He did well: *Hollywood Reporter* put him on its Next Gen Top 35 Under 35 and his career started to move – rather more sharply than did that of his then girlfriend, at least to begin with. LL Cool J nicknamed him Trevity-Trev-Trev, a moniker Meghan began using for her beau. The two were happy in the beginning and were to stay together for some time.

But while not quite matching the heights of her new boyfriend, at that stage at least, Meghan's career did begin to get underway, albeit with a string of fairly small roles. Her next appearance, in 2005, was as Cori in an episode of the *One on One* spinoff *Cuts* called 'My Boyfriend's Back': this was a comedy set in a hairdressing salon and for what it is worth, most of the cast was African American. This series was a little bit more successful than *Century City*: the thirty-one episodes ran from February 2005 to May 2006 and its cancellation was mainly due to the fact that the network UPN, on which it originally aired, merged with WB to form The CW. Not that it would have made much difference to Meghan, given that she was in just the one episode.

At times it could be dispiriting. Life was tough as a young actress and Meghan reflected this years later after she had found success in *Suits*. Asked what her advice would be to a young woman starting out in the profession, she told Matchesfashion.com, 'Don't give it five minutes if you're not going to give it five years. Really assess if it's what you want, and when you decide to give it a proper go, resolve to stick with it. Give it a shot before giving up – especially in this industry, which can be incredibly hard on your spirit.' On another occasion she told TV Choice, 'Quite honestly, you do so many pilots as an actor. I mean, first you try to get work and then you do pilots. I had done six that hadn't been picked up.'

However, despite all that she was beginning to attract some attention. That same year she was cast in her first film, *A Lot Like Love*, starring Ashton Kutcher, Amanda Peet and Taryn Manning, but it would be misleading to say she played a very large role – rather, her part was known as 'Hot Girl'. No matter. The film, which was all about a young couple who become friends but don't realise they are in fact the perfect couple until the final scene, was a clunker: 'That's weird. I'm sure that *When*

Harry Met Sally had been made already. And didn't it used to be funny?' asked *The Times*. 'The only reason I was rooting for them to get together was that they would both be off the market,' opined Richard Roeper of *Ebert & Roeper*. Perhaps it was just as well that Meghan's character didn't actually have a name.

There followed another one-off appearance in a television series, this time *Love, Inc.*, in which she played Teresa Santos in an episode entitled 'One on One' (no relation to the parent series of *Cuts*). *Love, Inc.* was another fairly short-lived series, running on UPN from September 2005 to May 2006 and revolving around a dating agency, but again, while it didn't set the world on fire, it kept the wolf from the door and was giving Meghan more acting experience.

In 2006 there was more of the same. There was another one-off appearance in another short-lived television series, *The War at Home*, in which Meghan appeared as a character called Susan in 'The Seventeen-Year Itch'. This one was a sitcom about a dysfunctional Long Island family and managed to last two seasons but it, too, failed to set the world alight.

That was followed by a made-for-television film *Deceit*, an attempt at a film noir, in which Meghan appeared in a minor role and which also failed to make any impact. Her next outing was at least in something that was considerably better established: a role in the long-running crime drama *CSI: NY*, in which she played Veronica Perez in an episode called 'Murder Sings The Blues'. It dealt with the topic of biological attack, but once more, this was a one-off and Meghan's role was a fairly fleeting one.

There was another two-year gap before another appearance in a television movie in 2008's *Good Behaviour*. At least this time Meghan had a considerably bigger role – but her big breakthrough was still some way away yet. It was essentially a remake of *Outrageous Fortune* and concerned a matriarch of a criminal family who decides it's time for her clan to go straight. Yet the fact that it still proved not to be that all-elusive breakthrough was clearly beginning to make Meghan think she might look elsewhere for a role in life.

And so it was that like so many aspiring actresses before her, Meghan took on other roles to keep herself going as she sought to make her name, including one that she appeared rather embarrassed about in later years. In 2007 she appeared on the second season of *Deal or No Deal*, which had premiered on NBC a couple of years previously and which starred The Models and The Banker: she was Briefcase Model number 26, one of numerous leggy beauties standing around holding a case which may or may not contain a lot of money. Promo shots from the time showed her in a low-cut, tight-fitting short red dress teamed with vertiginous heels; it was not a job she enjoyed and she left at the end of the season.

'I would put that in the category of things I was doing while I was auditioning to try to make ends meet,' she told *Esquire*, revealing quite how depressed the whole episode had made her. 'I went from working in the US Embassy in Argentina to ending up on *Deal*. It's run the gamut. Definitely working on *Deal or No Deal* was a learning experience, and it helped me to understand what I would rather be doing. So if that's a way for me to gloss over that subject, then I will happily shift gears into something else.'

It was certainly one of the cheesiest roles she took on and raised a few eyebrows when her relationship with Harry became public, albeit of the amused rather than scandalised variety. 'I didn't ever have it [the winning suitcase],' said Meghan, sounding like a pretty good sport. 'I don't think I did. I was the ill-fated number 26, which for some reason no one would ever choose. I would end up standing up there forever in these terribly uncomfortable and inexpensive five-inch heels, just waiting for someone to pick my number so I could go and sit down.' She returned to it in conversation with presenter Piers Morgan: 'I was a briefcase girl on *Deal or No Deal*... I cringe when I think about it now, but it paid the rent.'

Nevertheless, these somewhat unhappy experiences aside, her profile continued to grow among the cognoscenti, if not actually the public. There was another appearance in a very high-profile television series, *90210*, and this time her character, Wendy, appeared in two episodes, 'The Jet Set' and 'We're Not In Kansas Anymore'. In fact, she was busy that year: she also played Tara in an episode of another comedy titled *'Til Death* called *Joy Ride*. Then it was on to another TV movie called *The Apostles*, which was another cop drama and another instantly forgotten outing. But again, it was more to chalk up to experience.

In 2008 there was a new series of *Knight Rider*, based on both the famous series in the 1980s that made a star out of David Hasselhoff and more recent TV movie. It starred Justin Bruening as Mike Traceur, the estranged son of Michael Knight, and only lasted for one season, with Meghan playing the role of Annie Ortiz in the first episode. In the role she was forced to become a cage fighter, determined to find out the truth about her drill sergeant's death and, in a move that was bound to have gone down well with male viewers, forced to fight with another woman. She wore a skimpy black top in the process, another nod to male viewers, no doubt.

But matters soon picked up after that. Following an appearance in another cop show, *Without a Trace*, in which she played Holly Shepard in an episode called 'Chameleon', she got the role of junior FBI agent Amy Jessup in the very considerably more successful series *Fringe*. Indeed, for a short time it seemed as if this might be her breakthrough, and it is one of Meghan's projects that is frequently brought up as an example of her better past work. Initially the role was to have been a recurring one, although in the event, this turned out not to be the case.

Fringe, which was to run for five years, was a science-fiction series created by, among others, J. J. Abrams, who has worked on the more recent manifestations of *Star Trek* and *Star Wars*, alongside Alex Kurtzman, another well-respected film and television writer, producer and director, and his long-time collaborator, another highly successful television producer, Roberto Orci. It involved the work of three detectives who were members of the Fringe Division of the FBI, based in Boston, Massachusetts, investigating mysteries concerning parallel universes and various twilight zones. The three concerned were Olivia Dunham (Anna Torv), Peter Bishop (Joshua Jackson) and Walter Bishop (John Noble).

Fringe, in fact, established quite the cult following and had Meghan had a more substantial role, she might well have made her breakthrough rather sooner. It was a direct successor to the likes of *Lost*, *The X-Files*, *Altered States* and the *Twilight Zone* and it lasted long enough to evolve, moving from an episodic structure, in which there was one mystery per episode, to longer, arching storylines that helped form the parallel universe it was to create. Abrams also cited author Michael Crichton and film-maker David Cronenberg as inspirations.

It was not long before the show developed a cult following and many involved were nominated for numerous awards; the series also inspired two comic book series, three novels and an alternative-reality game. As the series advanced, various leitmotifs came to the fore: an alternative universe in which the September 11 terrorist attacks took place but where the Twin Towers in New York were left untouched – indeed, several of the episodes were set in the South Tower – and the mysterious glyph code, which enthralled many viewers. 'It's something we're doing for people who care to figure it out and follow it, but it's not something that a viewer has to consider when they watch the show,' Abrams said. The glyph symbols would appear in the opening sequence, alongside words such as 'dark matter' and 'teleportation'.

It went down pretty well with the critics. Barry Garron at *Hollywood Reporter* liked it because 'it is reminiscent of battle-of-the-sexes charm'; Robert Bianco, of *USA Today*, said, 'What Abrams brings to *Fringe* is a director's eye for plot and pace, a fan's love of sci-fi excitement, and a story-teller's gift for investing absurd events with real emotions and relatable characters.' Tim Goodman of the *San Francisco Chronicle* remarked that it was 'boundlessly ambitious' and *Chicago Sun-Times*'s Misha Davenport called it an 'update of *The X-Files* with the addition of terrorism and the office of Homeland Security.' But Meghan's breakthrough role it was not. She was continuing to struggle on and pay her dues – and it would be a few years before success finally came her way.

In other words, it was exactly the sort of show that could provide a launchpad for an aspiring actress, but as so often with everything in life, it did not go according to plan. The role did not last quite as long as had been initially hoped. 'That role was always crafted as being recurring or a series regular,' Meghan told BuzzFeed years later when she really had finally made her name. 'Akiva Goldsman was directing those first two episodes, and he'd been doing all that *DaVinci Code* stuff [Goldsman wrote the screenplays for *The Da Vinci Code* and *Angels &*

Demons], so this idea of how science and religion coexist was very much in the zeitgeist. I think it ended up being a storyline that scared off the studio or network, so Amy just evaporated. I was intending on being [in Vancouver, where *Fringe* filmed after moving from New York] for a while, but she was just phased out. Amy maintains this air of mystery and I kind of think fans assumed she was going to pop back up again – like Amy was the one behind all of the *Fringe* mysteries.'

Amy didn't pop back up again. But this had been a significant step up in Meghan's career and, interestingly, took her briefly to Canada, which is where she was going to spend so much of her professional life in the coming years. And for all that failure to land a recurring role in *Fringe* was a disappointment, it was a temporary one. Meghan had been paying her dues and it wouldn't be long now before she got the break for which she had fought so hard for so long.

CHAPTER 4

FAME AWAITS

And so, it was back on the road again. Meghan's personal life was going well, with her relationship with Trevor Engelson strengthening, but it was a return to the round of one-off appearances, pilots that went nowhere, and the endless frustrations that went with trying to make a breakthrough in the hugely competitive world of acting. Meghan was in her late twenties now, young by most standards, but not so much so in the world of films and television when you have still not made your mark. It did happen, of course, that older women went on to make a go of it – Kim Cattrall appeared in many films and television series before taking on the role of Samantha in *Sex and the City* in her early forties, which catapulted her into a new league – but time was passing and Meghan had yet to see any real success. And to have come so near and yet so far with the possibility of a recurring role in *Fringe* simply highlighted the fact that she was not yet where she wanted to be.

But she persevered. Her next role was another one-off, in an episode of *The League*, a long-running ensemble comedy that followed a group of friends in a fantasy football league, called The Bounce Test, in which she played a character imaginatively called Megan. Still no breakthrough. Next up was a small part in a Robert Pattinson movie called *Remember Me*: it was a cheery little tale centring on a pair of lovers, one of whom has witnessed her mother's murder and the other whose parents split up in the wake of his brother's suicide, and it was the first of a couple of projects in which she participated that attracted a great deal of attention due to the high profile of the leading man.

Meghan played an extremely small part, a character who rejoices in the name of Megan, while Meghan's boyfriend, Trevor Engelson was one of its producers. It attracted a fair bit of attention on the back of Robert Pattinson's involvement; he was then at the height of his *Twilight* fame and the stuff of tabloid fodder due to his then relationship with Kristen Stewart – giving Meghan a glimpse from afar of what a very high-profile relationship could look like – but the critics were pretty lukewarm.

'People meet, maybe they fall in love, maybe they don't, maybe they're happy, maybe they're sad. That's life. If, let us say, a refrigerator falls out of a window and squishes one of them, that's life, too, but it's not a story many people want to see,' wrote Roger Ebert, while giving it three stars out of four. 'I cared about the characters. I felt for them. Liberate them from the plot's destiny, which is an anvil around their necks, and you might have something [but it] tries to borrow profound meaning, but succeeds only in upstaging itself so overwhelmingly that its characters become irrelevant.'

Of course none of this was really relevant to Meghan, who was still in the situation of being a young actress paying her dues. Barely pausing for breath, she did another *CSI*, this time in Miami, where she played Officer Leah Montoya in an episode called 'Backfire', in which the team tried to work out the true story behind a fatal house fire. Meghan's role was low-key to the point of almost irrelevance, but at least she didn't have to stand around in high heels holding a briefcase, as she had in *Deal or No Deal*!

From there it was on to the film *Get Him to the Greek*, which also attracted attention on the back of a high-profile star, in this case Russell Brand. He was also enjoying a peak in his popularity and, like Pattinson, was in a very high-profile relationship, in this case courtesy of his brief marriage to the singer Katy Perry. A sequel to *Forgetting Sarah Marshall* – both films were written and directed by Nicholas Stoller and both starred Russell Brand and Jonah Hill – Brand appeared once more as the rock star Aldous Snow, who this time round was put under the supervision of an intern charged with getting him to the Greek Theatre.

The film received fairly positive reviews: 'under the cover of slapstick, cheap laughs, raunchy humor, gross-out physical comedy and sheer exploitation, *Get Him to the Greek* also is fundamentally a sound movie,' wrote Roger Ebert, giving it three stars. 'This is Brand's film and every aspect of his persona is played to the max – the sexual magnetism, the multiple addictions, the doting but distant mum, the hangers-on and the women who want to control him,' opined Tom Seymour in *Little White Lies*, but Meghan's role as Tatiana was so small it was actually uncredited. Time to move on.

As Meghan herself was later to remark, the work she did at that point was actually mainly comedy – something that surprised many when she went on to make her name in a drama series – although her roles were so small she wasn't given the chance to make much of an impact. But there were dramas, too, including the role of Kat in a nineteen-minute short called *The Candidate* in which, according to IMDb.com, 'An underhanded company man is offered assistance by a secret organisation that immerses him in forces beyond his control.' Her co-stars were Robert Picardo and Tom Gulager, and although her role was bigger than the productions she had previously been appearing in, the project itself was not enough to command much attention. It was only diehard Meghan fans, who started to appear when she first found television fame, who really remembered it in the longer term.

Meghan had a bigger role too in her next project, a curiosity called *The Boys & Girls Guide to Getting Down*. Originally an award-winning independent film directed by Paul Sapiano in 2006, Sapiano remade it for television, with the same plot and the same title, casting Meghan in one of the leading roles, that of Dana. It was a look at the twenty-something party lifestyle, broken down into episodic chapters and addressing such unprincessy subjects as drugs, clubs, alcohol and one-night stands. It was essentially a coming-of-age drama but an insubstantial one, for all of the attractive cast trying their best to stand out.

As interest in Meghan mounted in later years, one

ingenious fan put together a list of her best (and worst) films, inviting fellow fans to rate them by popular vote. *The Boys & Girls Guide* came in at number four out of eleven (number one was *The Apostles*, two was *The Candidate* and eleven was *Random Encounters*, of which more shortly); and in this raunchy little number lasting an hour and a half, she was generally held to have acquitted herself well.

One problem that she was to encounter on more than one occasion was caused by the fact that Meghan was mixed race, which ironically meant she would sometimes end up being either 'not black enough' or 'not white enough' for a particular role. 'I could get into twice as many rooms, but was turned down twice as often as many of my peers,' she told *Ebony* magazine. 'It's that dichotomy that we can go through: "What are you? Where do you fit in? I want to put you in this box and I want you to stay there." I never want to complain. I get that so many people have it worse than I do. But it took me deep into my twenties to come to the realisation that I am "enough" exactly as I am, and I don't have to be more or less of anything for other people.'

The next project saw her slipping down the cast list again, but to compensate it was a much bigger and more high-profile film. *Horrible Bosses* starred such luminaries as Jason Bateman, Kevin Spacey, Jennifer Aniston, Charlie Day, Jason Sudeikis, Colin Farrell and Jamie Foxx. It was a very successful and very black comedy about three friends, Bateman, Day and Sudeikis, who decide to murder their horrible bosses, played by Spacey, Aniston and Farrell, in a sort of take on the Hitchcock classic *Strangers on a Train*, in which the various parties concerned agree to commit murders for each other on the grounds that the killer would have no motive and would thus not be identified. The film did exceptionally well, achieving a wide release in July 2011, making over $28 million in the three days after opening and eventually going on to gross over $209 million worldwide, making it the highest-grossing black comedy of all time and breaking the previous record held by *The War of the Roses*.

Although there were carps at the dark subject matter, on the whole it received positive reviews. It was a film that sharply divided opinion, but Meghan had only a very small role as the FedEx girl Jamie, although there was certainly no shame in that – the great comedian Bob Newhart made a cameo appearance, while Donald Sutherland, no less, played a minor part. It certainly threw her in with the A-list: 'I met all of the cast and they're great,' she told Beamly.com, although there was a hint that this had also been forecast to be a much larger role and so there had been yet another disappointment there too. 'It's funny because with films like that they cut a lot, I mean I'm only in one scene but everyone is just nice,' she continued. 'People often forget that actors are real people. Just because I have a fancy job doesn't mean I'm fancy, we are still all normal.'

The year 2011 was in fact to be quite an eventful one for Meghan. It was when TV series *Suits* started to air and it was also the year she got married to her long-term boyfriend, Trevor Engelson, on 10 September, having got engaged the previous year. The two got hitched at Jamaica Inn in Ocho Rios, Jamaica, a long-time favourite destination of Meghan's, in front of 102 guests; the pair had been a couple now for six years and Meghan, barefoot, was glowing in a stunning white dress. The setting was pure romance: Jamaica Inn is an achingly luxurious resort perched on the edge of the Caribbean; very A-list and very chic and very much the sort of destination Meghan would come to be associated with.

A couple of years later – ironically, shortly before the couple separated – Meghan spoke of her love of the place to the *Chicago Tribune*. 'It's from the 1950s and is the spot where I got married,' she said of the Jamaica Inn. 'It's just old-school Hollywood and is so romantic. Marilyn Monroe and Arthur Miller used to have romantic jaunts there. It's the only place I've ever cried when I had to leave. We just took over the whole place [for the wedding]. It's tiny, but really special. I think there are tons of things you can do around the area but, for me, it's just nice to go and lay around and eat awesome food and spend time in the ocean. I'm all for cultural experiences, but when you need a little rest and relaxation, this is 100 per cent the place that I want to go to.'

The marriage was not to last, not least because of the pressures of carrying on a long-distance relationship, for Meghan was not only flitting around the world filming, she was now also spending much of the year in Canada filming *Suits*. Her own A-list moment was approaching but there was still a way to go. In 2012, a year after *Suits* began, of which much more in the next chapter, Meghan had another small role, that of Terry in a film called *Dysfunctional Friends*. It was an Agatha Christie-esque outing about nine estranged friends who are gathered at the estate of a deceased chum: they are told that they must spend five days together if they wish to receive an inheritance and that if so much as a single person leaves, then the inheritance is toast. All have dark secrets and tensions are not slow to emerge.

Dysfunctional Friends was an independent film, produced by Datari Turner and written and directed by Corey Grant. It became a cult hit and the reviews were generally favourable: 'Corey Grant is remarkably generous to his large cast, giving them juicy roles as a writer and, as a director, the space to run with them,' wrote Michael Dequina in TheMovieReport.com, while Wilson Morales in BlackFilm.com opined, 'Filled with humorous scenes along with some tender moments, Friends should attract an audience looking to have a good time and enjoy an evening's entertainment.' Not everyone liked it though: 'In addition to being crowded and over long, the pic is thoroughly unpleasant,' snarked John Anderson in *Variety*.

As her profile began to rise, Meghan found herself increasingly in demand. The days of filming numerous pilots that went nowhere were coming to an end and the projects she found herself caught up in were well thought of and well received. Her next appearance was in the popular and long-running detective series *Castle*: the premise was that the successful mystery writer Richard 'Rick' Castle (Nathan Fillion) turns detective when a serial killer begins to copy the plots of his novels. Meghan appeared in an episode entitled 'Once Upon A Crime' as Charlotte Boyd/Sleeping Beauty, in which three women are targeted, all dressed in costumes from the same shop as fairy-tale characters: Red Riding Hood, Snow White and Sleeping Beauty, although only the last of these survives. It also emerges that all three had recently drawn the same amount of money from their bank accounts: could it be that they were being blackmailed about a hit-and-run they committed as college classmates?

That May, after just twenty months of marriage, Meghan and Trevor quietly separated and were later to divorce, citing 'irreconcilable diffierences'. The couple kept it as low-profile as they could. Meghan didn't hire a lawyer, the case was uncontested and she waived her right to spousal support, while the pair followed common practice by appointing a temporary judge to rule on their affairs. Neither has spoken publicly about what happened, although there were rumours – hotly contested – that Meghan had become too close to the Canadian ice-hockey star Michael Del Zotto. Everyone involved point-blank denied there was any intimacy between the two and a close source said that the two had never actually been alone together, but it was the case that two pictures had been posted on social media showing the two together after Meghan had watched him playing with the New York Rangers. Meghan called him 'the best'.

A friend revealed, 'Trevor was devastated at the split. She suddenly had no time for him. She said she was just friends with Michael. Her social media had pics and references to him but she deleted it all after divorcing.' Trevor himself was asked about Del Zotto: 'Who? Oh, him,' he replied. 'I don't have anything to say about it. I just can't.' Whatever the reason behind the split, Meghan was on the market once more.

It was to be several years before she met her handsome prince, but Meghan was a very attractive woman, newly single, and there was no shortage of suitors. She did not go public about anyone, however, and so speculation was rife as to the true state of her romantic life which, ironically, gave her something else in common with Harry, who had spoken openly of the difficulty in forming a relationship because every woman he was pictured with was immediately spoken of as a potential future wife.

Meghan was in a very similar position. In 2014 the golfer Rory McIlroy nominated her to do the Ice Bucket Challenge, the craze that went around the world when people nominated others to have a bucket full of ice and water thrown over them in order to bring attention to the ALS Association: she accepted on condition that Rory himself threw the bucket over her (and she, in turn, nominated Serena Williams). The video made of the event shows the two of them larking about together and Meghan practically breathless with laughter after getting soaked; their obvious chemistry and the fact that they were spotted having dinner together in a Dublin restaurant soon afterwards gave manner to all sorts of speculation, but the two of them were never more than friends.

In fact Meghan had met a new man: the Canadian restaurateur Cory Vitiello, who bore a slight resemblance to Trevor Engelson and ran a chain of restaurants in Toronto (where her show *Suits* was filmed). The relationship was serious enough for them to move into a townhouse together, near a park where they would walk their dogs, Guy and Bogart. Meghan was clearly smitten, even if it proved to be temporary: in an interview with *Esquire* she commented, 'The best job a man could have would be a chef. They'd understand the hours I work and the drive and ambition it takes to succeed.' She was a real foodie, too, which meant the two had a great deal in common.

Cory, according to Meghan's website, The Tig, of which more anon, had trained at the Stratford Chef Academy and founded a catering company out of the family home in Brantford, Ontario. He went on to open an extremely popular Toronto restaurant called The Harbord Room, now closed, a tiny establishment which went from neighbourhood favourite to one of the best-known eateries in the city, and from there founded a chain called Flock, which specialised in chicken.

He became quite a local celebrity himself: 'There's no downside to being a well-known chef,' he told *Toronto Life*. 'There are thousands of great cooks in the city, and there are chefs who are more deserving of the celebrity [label] than myself. It's a very fortunate time to be a chef in Toronto, with the huge public interest and the growing number of job opportunities outside of the kitchen. There's definitely a glamorisation of the industry that doesn't match the reality.'

Meghan was also extremely busy with her professional life. For the first time, rather than people noticing her because of the film she was in, the focus started to shift and people began to notice the film because Meghan was in it. Her roles got bigger, although due to the time commitment in filming *Suits*, she wasn't doing quite as much elsewhere as previously. And all that said, her choices were not universally good ones. In 2013 she played a lead in a rather misjudged outing called *Random Encounters* opposite Sean Young and Michael Rady: it was the story of a chance encounter between two people in a coffee shop, which led to a full-on romance that faced many obstacles along the way. It was a he-said, she-said kind of narrative, set in the world of Los Angeles showbiz, and in truth it didn't really work and the film went nowhere.

Outside *Suits* her next project was another TV movie, *When Sparks Fly*, except that unfortunately they didn't. The story concerned Amy, played by Meghan, a journalist working in the big city, who is sent back to her home town to write a fourth of July story. While there, she somewhat predictably begins to learn about all that she has been missing in life. She is asked by a friend to help arrange her wedding, which just happens to be to Amy's ex... The film was shown on the Hallmark Channel but was generally felt to have been one of their less successful offerings.

Nor was her next project a huge success. *Anti-Social* was in fact a rather surprising film for Meghan to appear in, not least as it was about the gangster community in London, a sort of poor-man's Guy Ritchie-fest. Written and directed by Reg Traviss, who was once engaged to Amy Winehouse, it followed the story of two brothers, Dee, a street artist, and Marcus, an armed robber. Dee becomes well known for his work while Marcus grows rich on the proceeds of crime, but then a gang war erupts and both the police and rival gangsters close in. Meghan's part was as an American model (she wasn't called on to hazard a British accent) called Kirsten who falls in love with Dee. It was based on three real-life London crimes: the 2009 Graff diamonds robbery, the 2012 Brent Cross shopping centre smash and grab, and the 2013 robbery of Selfridges, which was carried out by men wearing burkas.

The film wasn't a great success and the reviews reflected that. 'Lairy geezer action sits awkwardly alongside dreary discussions of the politics of street art in writer/director Reg Traviss's uninspiring crime caper,' wrote Mark Kermode in *The Observer*. 'Traviss is clearly searching for cockney cool and "lots of layers, like life" but can't find either in the one-note flimsiness of the plastic plot that's worsened by weak ensemble acting,' opined Alan Jones in the *Radio Times*. 'A painful slog through geezer-thriller terrain,' was the opinion of Simon Crook in *Empire* magazine, while Leslie Felperin in *The Guardian* wrote, 'It's essentially constructed from crime-film clichés that could claim a pension and, worst of all, it's way too long.' Kate Muir was a little nicer about it in *The Times*: 'The film displays remarkable energy and fun, although the London gangster milieu and its "blud 'n' bruv" slang is overused,' she wrote.

(When the film first came out, it made very little impact, being released in just forty cinemas across the UK. But Traviss was nothing if not a pragmatist and when the news about Meghan and Harry emerged, he re-edited the film and released it again for digital download and screening – this time greatly enhancing her role.

She was accorded second billing, after Gregg Sulkin, who played Dee, and also featured heavily in the three-minute trailor, in which she was shown emerging from a shower, drinking champagne and modelling perfume as well as featuring in a steamy bedroom scene. Reg said he wanted to 'delve deeper into one of the storylines... a shorter, more compact version of the original' – although, of course, taking advantage of the fact that one of his actresses was all over the papers because she was dating a Prince of the Realm couldn't hurt.)

Even before the news of the relationship with Prince Harry broke, however, her star was very much in the ascendant and as such she got another lead role in another TV movie for the Hallmark Channel: *Dater's Handbook*. It was about a successful businesswoman with a duff love life who, with her sister's encouragement, turns to a dating handbook by the relationships expert Dr Susie and links up with several potential suitors to try out the guide. Somewhat inevitably, she ends up having to choose between 'reliable George and fun-loving Robert'. Meghan played Cass, the businesswoman in question, and it was generally conceded that, charming as she was on screen, this wasn't going to set the world on fire.

CHAPTER 5

SUITS

Television is an intensely competitive industry, as Meghan knew better than most. She had been at the coal face, as it were, seeing any number of potentially exciting projects being launched and then going nowhere fast. But she was finally going to get the opportunity she had been waiting for in a legal drama, a show that was to make her a star well before any princes came on the scene. Indeed, it was to provide a launchpad into a new life that would see her become not just a well-known actress, but a respected activist, lifestyle blogger and entrepreneur.

Her star began to rise at the start of the second decade of the twenty-first century. It was April 2010, and the USA Network had announced details of seven pilots for new drama series, including one with the working title *A Legal Mind*. Not a great deal of information was forthcoming: the network merely announced that the new offering from executive producers David Bartis and Gene Klein 'centers on a college dropout who has to navigate the corporate world while attempting to grow up.'

The show's creator was Aaron Korsh, who already had a very successful career in television behind him, writing for such notables as *Everybody Loves Raymond*, *Just Shoot Me!*, *Love, Inc.* and *Notes from the Underbelly*, and it was he who wrote the pilot. It was initially conceived as a 'half-hour *Entourage*-type based on my experiences working on Wall Street', but he soon realised that the project merited something considerably more, and after doing the rounds of a series of production companies, met with Alex Sepiol, a USA Network executive, who gave it the green light. Hypnotic Films & Television came on board and after a rewrite and rethink about the profession in which it should be set, gave it the go-ahead.

The drama was originally to be set in the world of finance, but moved to the legal profession because no professional requirements are needed for working on Wall Street, whereas they are required in law, an essential point in the premise of the show. Set in the fictional New York law firm Pearson Hardman, *Suits* centres on two men: Mike Ross (Patrick J. Adams), who has a photographic memory, a brilliant legal mind and takes legal exams for other people, but, despite pretending otherwise, has never attended law school, and Harvey Specter (Gabriel Macht), a senior partner at the firm. Harvey knows Mike's secret, but hires him anyway because of his brilliant legal mind. Other important characters included Jessica Pearson (Gina Torres), the co-founder and managing partner of the firm; Rachel Zane (Meghan), a paralegal who becomes romantically involved with Mike and who wishes to become a lawyer herself; Louis Litt (Rick Hoffman), like Harvey, a Harvard graduate – and Harvey's rival – and in charge of first-year associates; and Donna Paulsen (Sarah Rafferty), Harvey's secretary and close confidante and the only other person who knows Mike's secret. It was essentially a six-person ensemble cast, although of course there were many other recurring characters, too, not least Trevor Evans (Tom Lipinski), Mike's closest friend, who is also a drugs dealer. A later, important introduction to the cast was Daniel Hardman (David Costabile), the other founding partner until Jessica had him removed after finding out he'd been embezzling.

The concept was already so well thought out that few changes had to be made. 'The first half-hourish is pretty much, with small tweaks, as it was then,' Korsh told *The Hollywood Reporter*. 'He (Mike) didn't take LSATs [Law School Admission Council tests] for people, he was just a super smart guy. Though when he gets hired, it's basically the same. It was interesting because when it's Wall Street, he was only faking going to Harvard, he wasn't faking a law degree. To work on Wall Street, to be a mathematical genius, there is no degree you need to have whereas to practise [law], you need to pass the bar. We decided to embrace and use it.'

There were certain challenges when it came to setting the show in a law firm, although in fairness, the same would have applied had it been set on Wall Street. 'The first few episodes, we had to rework the outlines several times,' Korsh explained. 'The challenge is, you've got a corporate law firm but you don't want your clients to be hateful. The challenge was to figure out how to credibly give us sympathetic clients without making it seem unrealistic that this type of law firm would take those types of clients. It took us a couple of cracks to do that. Sometimes we had to abandon how we constructed the first couple of episodes.'

Patrick – who Meghan already knew from previous casting sessions – was signed first as Mike, followed shortly afterwards by Gabriel as Harvey. The others began to come on board, with Meghan at long last getting the break she had been waiting for when she joined the cast in August, the last of the major roles to be filled. 'The show is based on the idea that this one guy has a legal mind, and the show was actually called *A Legal Mind* before it was renamed to *Suits*, and Mike Ross is the character who is a Mensa of sorts but is a little rough around the edges,' Meghan told *Female First* some years later.

'He ends up working at a law firm even though he is not a lawyer. The first series follows his relationship with Harvey Specter, who is one of the most prominent lawyers in Manhattan, and how Mike Ross is trying to keep this secret of not truly being a lawyer but having the mind of one and trying to find his way in this world. Of course with the help of many characters in the show but especially my character Rachel Zane he finds an ally and together they work through many of these cases – and of course there is a little bit of a love interest in all of that.'

In actual fact, Meghan initially thought that she hadn't got the part and was touchingly pleased that the show called for her character to have brains as well as beauty. 'When I read the pilot script and I went in to audition for it, I thought I blew my audition,' she told *Marie Claire*. 'I remember leaving, calling my agent, and saying, "I don't think I did a good job in that room, and I need to get back in there." So automatically, Rachel and I are very similar: ambitious, driven, and always trying to take the bull by its horns. My agent just said, "There's nothing I can do. Just focus on your next audition." This was not realising that behind the scenes, they loved my audition, and were putting together a test deal for me. And again, maybe that's where I'm similar to Rachel, in that I'm harder on myself than anyone else might be. I will say that working in the Embassy has rooted my performance for this in a different way. I love the intelligence that's written into Rachel. Look, my very first audition was for "Hot Girl #1" in some movie. It's the ultimate for me that the writers are able to go "Sure, you can be a pretty girl, but there's so much more to her.'"

That said, although Meghan's character is indeed brainy and intelligent, it was accepted right from the outset that she did not look like the back end of a bus. From the moment she swishes on camera in her opening scene, in which she is introduced to Mike, and indeed the audience, all flicky hair and confident stride, the audience is aware that she's a glamour puss. Her opening remark is to tell Mike not to hit on her, which he does anyway, and much play is made of the fact that he's ogling her rather than listening to her explain the intricacies of the firm, only for him to reveal that he knows exactly what she's just said, due to that photographic memory.

Rachel Zane's backstory is this: her father, Robert Zane, is a brilliant lawyer and partner of Rand, Kaldor & Zane. Despite the family's wealth, Rachel works to support herself but due to an inability – eventually overcome – to get an LSAT high enough for a top university on the grounds that she freezes when taking exams – ironic, as Mike has been taking LSATs for other people – she is working as a paralegal. Nonetheless, she is well respected by the firm, which sees her as one of its more competent employees, and when she does finally get into Columbia, continues to work part-time for the firm. Initially determined not to enter into a relationship with a co-worker, on the grounds that one such venture previously ended in disaster, she is eventually won round and ultimately falls in love and gets engaged to Mike.

Robert Zane himself reawoke some of the issues Rachel had to deal with earlier in life. He is played by Wendell Pierce, who is black, and there was an unpleasant reaction to their casting from some members of the public online when the show first aired. 'There was a racist undercurrent,' Meghan told *The Star*. 'It was ugly online, upsetting, people saying she's not black, I thought she was hot. [She could be] a fly on the wall [about racism] because people can't immediately tell what my background is.'

Although most of the filming was to take place in Toronto, the ninety-minute pilot was shot in New York City, where the story was set. The first season, comprising twelve episodes, started on 23 June 2011 and finished on 8 September that year. This was to be a very different experience for Meghan from her earlier ventures in that *Suits*, as it was now known, was a resounding success. 'There's no shortage of character fodder here and the dialogue is snappy with a pop-culture flavor,' wrote David Hinckley in the *New York Daily News*. 'These stylish suits aren't empty, by any means,' opined Diane Werts in *Newsday*. 'The fun comes in watching the uncynical Adams learn to undercut everyone else's coming,' thought Tom Gliatto in *People* magazine. Not everyone was a fan, of course ('Rarely have I had as hard a time getting through an inflated USA pilot than I did through all 73 minutes of *Suits*,' grumbled Alan Sepinwall in *HitFix*), but it was a hit, a palpable hit.

No one who has not served their time doing the rounds of endless TV studios, getting their hopes raised and then dashed could imagine quite what elation and delight Meghan and the rest of the cast felt when they realised the series was a success and they were going to be big stars. Even so, it took quite a while for it all to sink in. 'I've done so many pilots that have never seen the light of day and we didn't know that *Suit*s was going to become huge at the time. So it's been such a good transition!' Meghan told *Glamour*. 'The first year, we were in such a bubble – the show wasn't airing in Canada and now, there's security and police and fans and tears when we're filming so it's been such a wild ride for all of us! They've asked us for seven seasons so we're going to be there for at least a couple more years. Toronto has been really good to us.'

At the time of writing, there have been six series of *Suits*, with developments including Rachel finding out about Mike's secret and becoming engaged to him; the world finding out Mike's secret and Mike ending up in jail; and huge changes in the firm, which is massively damaged by the revelation and which has now mutated into Pearson Specter Litt. Different cast members developed their own followings – Louis Litt, in particular, turned into a great favourite, with his love of cats and ballet leading people to make all sorts of assumptions about him. And while it is certainly too soon to be able to tell whether *Suits* will be seen as one of the all-time television greats, it is slick, sassy, well written and produced and capable of grabbing hold of the viewer and hanging on. It has received numerous nominations for awards, with Gina Torres and Patrick J. Adams singled out for outstanding performances, and has been shown on networks all over the world.

Of course, attention began to focus on the actors themselves, as well as the characters they played. Meghan had attracted a small amount of notice in the past, but nothing major. Now, however, she was one of the main characters in a very popular television series, young, pretty and sometimes single to boot, and she quite suddenly began to attract an awful lot of attention. She had always dressed well, but she had to grow up and find a more sophisticated style fast, because now she was on display, not just when she was papped out and about but also when she was seen out at events and award ceremonies.

'I think [my style has] really changed because my sensibility had always been relaxed California girl style, and on any given day I was in jeans, cut-offs and flip-flops. But the weather alone in Toronto changes your wardrobe!' Meghan told *Glamour* when she was asked about her personal style. 'The fashion on *Suits* is gorgeous, so it also became my education of designers and really knowing what fits my body well. Now what I'm starting to learn is, even though things look amazing on the hanger, it doesn't mean they're going to look amazing on me. For example, I love Victoria Beckham dresses, but I don't have the long torso to support that silhouette. I wear a lot of Burberry on the show, and I wear a lot of Prabal [Gurung], because Rachel's whole aesthetic is someone who comes from money and has a real classic design sensibility. It's really modern because she's still young.'

Tom Ford's designs featured strongly, too, she went on: '...because as all paralegals do, she [Rachel] wears a Tom Ford skirt to the office! It's so funny because girls come up to me on the street and they feel like they know you and they'll say, "Oh, what was that skirt that you were wearing last week?!" and I'll be like, "Well, A, I was wearing it seven months ago, and B, it was a Tom Ford skirt – so you want to know but you don't really want to know that it was a $5,000 skirt – and I don't get to keep it!" But it's been really cool to see what works for my body and what doesn't.'

Other facets of Meghan's personality were also coming to light. Her character, Rachel Zane, was very interested in food and it emerged that the producers decided that should be the case because it was also true of Meghan. In a forerunner of what was to become her lifestyle blog, The Tig, Meghan started tweeting food advice, and also spoke about it in *USA Today* in 2012: 'I love food,' she began. 'Unapologetically so. With long shooting hours for season two of USA's *Suits*, it's important to balance the decadent treats that make my heart go pitter pat, and the nourishment that fuels my body. My favorite foods run the gamut from healthy to indulgent, but rest assured, they are always delicious. Just like my character, Rachel Zane, I'm a foodie, so if I'm going to eat it, it has to be good.'

She went on to share a list of favourites, including watermelon and cinnamon, seasoned veggie quinoa, fish tacos, chicken adobo, kale chips and a delicious glass of wine. Of this last she spoke of recently campervanning through New Zealand with her then husband and finding obscure wineries – there was no sign at that stage that there was to be trouble in that particular paradise. Indeed, over and again Meghan was to emphasise her foodie credentials, although given her slim physique she clearly didn't spend all her time eating. Rather, as she also revealed, she was a big runner and practiced a lot of yoga.

And so Meghan's life formed into a pattern. For eight months of every year she was in Toronto filming *Suits* and the other four months would be divided between other acting projects (some of which have been described in the last chapter), travel and developing her other interests, of which more anon. The cast formed friendships, as well they might, spending so much time together. It was an easygoing, intimate set-up that Meghan described to *Esquire*: 'What we've been doing every year since we've been [filming *Suits* in Toronto] is [co-star] Patrick J. Adams and his family have us up to their home on an island on the Georgian Bay. [...] When we have a three-day holiday weekend, we all drive up there with our coolers and our beer, and everyone brings their kids and husbands and wives and everything.'

Meghan had also settled well into Toronto itself, luxuriating in the fact that it was a very foodie destination. 'It's a solid food scene,' she told Wdish.com. 'Coming from LA, I was worried about not being able to have all those same flavors I love so much and that level of dining, but it's very comparable in the melting pot of it all here, and how diverse Toronto is, which I love, especially being biracial, I love that there's so much culture and diversity.'

As the character of Rachel developed, so too did her sense of style, and Meghan repeatedly harked back to Rachel's clothes and what they said about her character. Indeed, like so many prominent women before her, she was to find that her clothes were in many ways a means of sending signals to the world as well as being able to develop an increasingly sophisticated style of her own.

What she wore these days made the papers and Meghan appreciated as much.

As her character encountered new scenarios as the show progressed, so too were progressions in her wardrobe required. In the early series of the show Rachel was almost entirely confined to the office, but as the plots expanded on her role and her relationship with Mike, that required her to be seen outside. And that in turn put further demands on her wardrobe. In an interview she revealed the full extent the wardrobe department went to, with no detail overlooked, using even the colour of her clothes to signify her moods.

'Well, it's only been in the past few seasons that we've seen Rachel off-duty, so that was a good question with wardrobe and our costume designer, [and] we thought about what I would wear,' Meghan told *Glamour*. 'A lot of it is about quality and classics – like the perfect cashmere sweater with relaxed jeans. She also wore a Canadian tuxedo – we saw her at home in that – and you get to see that as aspirational as her wardrobe is on the show, she's still a real person.

'Rachel's clothes reflect how she's feeling,' she went on, 'because that's what happens in real life, right? When she and Michael were falling in love, everything was a blush tone and it was creams and layers and she was happier, and when she was really stressed everything was darker and there were slate and black tones. And at the very beginning, she wore a lot of black, because I think that's what happens when you're younger and you want to be taken seriously – and then you lighten up, and your clothes reflect that.'

As with any successful long-running role, there was often confusion about who was Meghan and who was Rachel. Were they actually the same person? They certainly had a great deal in common, not least in that both were brainy lookers with a serious side and an interest in food. As Meghan became increasingly closely associated with her character, *Marie Claire* asked if it was tough being connected to her but having no say over her fate. 'I don't know if it's tough, but I would say that it's exciting,' she replied. 'For me, I see Rachel as such a good friend, and when you play a character you love, it's so much easier. I root for her; I'm almost like a fan. If I wasn't on the show, I would really love this show, because each of the characters is like someone you know.'

Another cause for confusion was the fact that their style and taste in clothing seemed to have fused into one. 'Rachel is like the ultimate best friend who has a closet that I always borrow things from in my personal life,' Meghan continued. 'Her clothes are amazing! Jolie

Andreatta, our wardrobe designer, and I have worked really hard to make Rachel's wardrobe believable and to make it more like a closet of a mid-twenties girl, who works, and yes, has these amazing pieces, but I always mix and match. I wear the skirt that I wore in the pilot so much. It's like pulling from your closet. All the jewelry that I wear on the show is my own personal jewelry and family heirlooms, like my grandma's charm bracelet and my signet ring.'

She took it even further on another occasion. 'We are both strong-willed and driven, as well as being layered and sensitive,' Meghan wrote in 2016. 'The difference between the two of us is that she certainly cries a lot more than I do, but for good reason. Her life is a tad more dramatic than mine, so I certainly can't judge. What do we have in common? Our ambition and our taste in shoes.'

In many ways it was ironic that Meghan made her name in a programme called *Suits*, because from then on that emphasis on her own appearance never let up. She was going to turn it to her own advantage, of course, with the launch of a clothing line, and she also accepted that this aspect of her interested people as much as anything else. She was also a quick learner, demonstrating a clued-up approach to fashion in more recent interviews than previously shown.

Asked (again) about her style, in fact she seemed very in the know. 'It's a lot more relaxed than Rachel's,' she told Matchesfashion.com. 'If I think about my style icons, I love [stylist] Géraldine Saglio, and [*Vogue Paris* editor] Emmanuelle Alt. The way I dress is really monochromatic or tonal, and I like really classic pieces. I also love that French way of styling, where if your outfit is pulled together, then something's got to be dishevelled – your hair, your make-up. Whereas with Rachel, everything is just polished and perfect. There's something really pretty about effortless beauty.'

As for more formal appearances, where all eyes are upon you, a mistake can flash around the world in seconds and linger over you for years: 'I used to try to wear what people told me looked great, as opposed to what I was comfortable in. Now, the designer I wear so often on the red carpet is Lanvin – just beautifully crafted, simple silhouettes. I wore this really beautiful, nude-coloured gown to the American Ballet Theatre opening, and it just fits me to a T. Wear what makes you comfortable, and isn't going to make you cringe in three years when you see the photo. I'm not very trend driven. I'll pepper it in here and there, but invest in classic pieces and you'll never regret it.'

So this was the new Meghan: assured, stylish, very

much a woman of her time. Whether or not her new relationship with Harry, and potential future status as a royal consort, will allow her to continue acting is another question entirely. But one thing is for sure, *Suits* has provided her with far more than just acting success: she has used her profile to branch out into many other areas, taken an active interest in women's issues and proved that she is far more than just a pretty face. She has become an impressive personality in her own right and a woman many people are happy to look up to. Much, in fact, like Rachel Zane.

CHAPTER 6

THE TIG

These days, actors do far more than just act. Many of them have become canny businesspeople, too, and become involved with the 'lifestyle' society, whereby their own gilded existences can be put to some kind of commercial profit. The advent of social media meant that big-name stars were able to establish a direct connection with their fans and followers, most obviously on sites such as Twitter and Instagram, but increasingly through projects of their own.

And while famous actresses and models had always been used in advertising and promotions, now they could take a far more direct approach. Since the inception of Gwyneth Paltrow's lifestyle site Goop in 2008, many more such sites and initiatives followed, some incorporating lifestyle advice and others straightforward businesses: Reese Witherspoon's Draper James lifestyle brand, Ellen DeGeneres' E.D. On Air business on QVC, Drew Barrymore's beauty brand Flower, Blake Lively's Preserve (now closed) and Jessica Alba's the Honest Company to name but a few. The power of celebrity harnessed to the ability to communicate directly to the consumer was revolutionising the retail world, to say nothing of producing many promotional platforms that ended up benefiting everyone involved.

And so it was no surprise that now Meghan found she had a profile of her own, she should think about a similar project. For a start, the constant emphasis on her appearance, as documented in the previous chapter, made her a very obvious person to listen to on the subject of clothes and beauty products: if she hadn't been an expert when she started filming *Suits*, she certainly was now. Meghan had a hinterland too, which included food, and it made her a pretty good role model; it was possible to eat and still look that good. And, like Gwyneth Paltrow before her, she had started out on Twitter, with lifestyle tips as well as personal observations, which had already built up quite a following. At the time of writing Meghan had just one 374,000 followers on Twitter compared to

94

Gwyneth's 3+ million, but that was still a massive reach and it made sense for her to take the next step. And so, in 2014, just three years after taking on the role in *Suits* that was to change her life, Meghan launched The Tig, a lifestyle website that capitalised on her own interests, encompassing beauty, lifestyle and food.

The Tig was a solid reflection of the person behind it. Meghan had never shied away from confronting issues of race – indeed, she was frequently the first to bring it up – but her public profile, which reflected the inner reality, was actually of a sun-dappled California girl, brought up in LA and now making her home for part of the year in more wintry Toronto. All the qualities of a California girl were on display: a laid-back, sunny nature, casual personal style which, due to her current circumstances, had sharpened up into a really elegant demeanour; a clean-living and healthy-eating persona; and all those years spent travelling the world were now to be put to good use, too. Meghan was actually an extremely appealing personality, to prince and commoner alike, and she had the ideal image to front the site.

She was good at seizing the moment too. Everyone who knew her knew that Meghan was far more than just a pretty face and now the rest of the world was about to find out. It appeared she also had a pretty canny business brain. 'A company approached me to start a website, but I figured that if I was going to start something that was an extension of me, it really needed to feel organic, so I decided to do it myself – I write all of the content myself in order to keep the content feeling authentic,' Meghan told *In Style*. 'I really wanted to start a site that's the "go-to" for everything – that's why I have insider travel guides, food posts from famous chefs, fashion with the guidance of the likes of Wes Gordon and Edie Parker, and beauty, which I am involved in a lot because of *Suits*.' It was to be the start of a major new project for her and a platform from which she could launch herself in numerous different ways.

In these days of über-branding, every detail counts. For a start, the choice of name for the website was telling and it referred not to fashion, but to the world of the gourmet; The Tig refers to one of Meghan's favourite wines. Meghan had a highly refreshing attitude to food and drink compared to many of her fellow actresses: while running and yoga kept her trim, she made no bones about the fact that she did not deny herself the finer things in life – far from it. 'Tignanello is a full-bodied red wine that I tried about seven years ago,' Meghan told the Tory Daily website around the time that her own website launched. 'In wine circles, it is nicknamed "Tig". It was my first moment of getting it – I finally understood what people meant by the body, structure, finish, legs of wine. The TIG is my nickname for me getting it. Not just wine, but everything.' That was something else that set her apart from many actresses – she was very vocal about her love of wine and how she would prefer a glass of something special to almost any sweet treat.

Her interview with the website, itself a showcase for the fashion designer Tory Burch, was a case in point of how her life was changing. She modelled Tory Burch clothes for the Tory Burch website while talking about her own new venture, upping both her own profile and theirs. It was another new twist on a classic combination: famous designer and famous actress team up; the beautiful clothes add to the actress's glamour, while the actress's glamour reflects back on the designer. Everyone was happy; both benefited and raised profiles were had by all.

And so, Meghan set about providing what really boils down to the Markle guide to life and she was adamant that the work, the reviews, the recommendations were all her own. She needed some assistance, of course, in running The Tig, but the website was hers and was a reflection of her life and what was important to her. 'I do what I can when I can,' she explained to Tory Daily of the balance she had to strike between her filming schedule and her new project. 'I write 100 per cent of the content – much in between scenes in my trailer or on weekends. I have someone helping with posts and emails and doing graphic design for certain posts. But the bulk of the photography and writing is my labour of love.'

To log on to The Tig is to log on to the sun-dappled world of Planet Markle. In the numerous photographs adorning the website, Meghan peers in a sultry fashion outside her trailer, alongside her dogs, or stares moodily into space. In every one she looks immaculate and in several she proves that she looks as good without her make-up as she does with it. Interviews with inspirational people are scattered everywhere, as is evidence of her campaigning activity, of which more later. Her personality shines through at every point, while her natural interests come to the fore.

As promised, the content reflected Meghan's life, interests and pastimes. Foremost among these were the gourmand tendencies that gave The Tig its name. 'Food was a no-brainer to me because I love to cook,' she told *InStyle*. 'I grew up gardening; I'm from California and farm-to-table is very much in our ethos. Beyond that, I work on a show that's so heavily fashion driven and has given me the opportunity to go to New York Fashion Weeks, which has really evolved my style from growing up in LA and wearing cutoffs and flip-flops to really wearing beautiful pieces and finding my own taste level, which I want to share with readers. For my beauty category, I didn't want to just do make-up and hair tips – it's really about the internal beauty, too. For my birthday, I did a post about being comfortable in your own skin.'

The upbeat tone of the interview reflected the fact that Meghan had finally achieved what she'd wanted, both in her professional life as an actress and the ways in which she was beginning to branch out. But while this was Planet Markle, it didn't tell the whole story. There was no hint of the sadness that lay behind her divorce nor indeed the fact that there was a new man on the scene – although The Tig ran many interviews with chefs and restaurant reviews including one of The Harbord Room, which Meghan commented was 'hands-down my absolute favorite restaurant in Toronto'. And why shouldn't it be? Her relationship with restauranteur Cory Vitiello was going just as well as everything else.

Meghan had spoken a lot about her love of travel in the past and so it was only natural that would play a major part in the new website, too. 'Travel is hugely important to me,' she told *InStyle*. 'My mom was a travel agent, so I've always loved off-the-beaten-track, indie, super cool places. I've always gotten requests from people who ask things like, "where should I eat in Bangkok?" or "where should I stay in Paris?" So I wanted to make this the go-to site for those insider-y type guides. I also want to know where the cool kids go, so I turn to people like interior designer Natasha Baradaran who wrote the *Insider's Guide to Milan* [for the site]. I am fortunate to travel a lot, so I want to share that as well – like my travels to Tulum [Mexico], where I took my new Tig bag!' And as such there was a series called Insider's Guide, which provided information on myriad destinations, everything from agreeable US neighbourhoods to some of the more obscure outposts of Bali. Meghan was proving she was just as well travelled as she'd always maintained, and trips, such as a couple of days in Vienna, provided further material for her postings. The tone was always cheery; the tips were always sound.

Back to the aforementioned Tig bag. This was another very obvious development on the site and another good example of the benefits of the cross promotion of several businesses: Meghan was sporting a specially commissioned clutch bag bearing the insignia of her website and of course information about where it came from. The bag in question was made by Edie Parker, a company that creates custom clutches, and the style Meghan opted for was of a pearlised hue with 'Ms

Tig' spelt out in glittery writing. The buying page was accompanied by a blog talking about the company and giving readers the information they needed to get a Ms Tig (or any other design) bag of their own.

Even at that early stage Meghan talked happily about embarking on further collaborations and it wasn't long before they were up and running: Birchbox, for example, a New York-based online monthly subscription service that sends subscribers a small box of make-up and beauty-related samples, created a Tig Birchbox containing various lotions and potions for the very reasonable sum of $10.

There followed Tig Tunes, in which music lists were curated by some of Meghan's favourite artists – the first one was Nikki Yanofsky, who chose numbers by Chet Baker, Amy Winehouse, Aretha Franklin, Stevie Wonder, Smokey Robinson, Leon Bridges and, of course, herself. It was beginning to look like a Tig world takeover. Tig Influencers was a forum in which high-profile women were asked about their likes and dislikes: subjects included the Indian actress Priyanka Chopra, editor-in-chief of *Good Housekeeping* Jane Francisco, actress Yara Shahidi, Moon Juice founder Amanda Chantal Bacon, tennis player Serena Williams and, as interest in her grew, Meghan herself.

It was just a matter of time before Meghan took the next logical step and launched her own clothing range as so many celebrities had done before her, which she did with a capsule collection in conjunction with Reitmans, which kicked off in 2015 and only ended in early 2017. Reitmans was a long-established Canadian clothing company, founded in 1926, with nearly 700 stories separated into six operating chains and a motto that could have been made for Meghan: 'Fits your beautiful'. The initial approach came from the company: bright, sassy Meghan was clearly an ideal fit for their store. Reitmans got in touch totally unexpectedly, she told Wdish.com, to ask if she'd like to put a new twist on old favourite styles: 'What excited me the most is that they wanted to really shake things up a little bit, and to re-energise… It feels really humbling, that they trust me with that [restyling the clothes]. That they would go, "Okay, here's the current collection; how do you see it?"' [They want] to make it so that when you're thinking about buying something new, you go, "Oh, I have a date" or "I have an interview; I'll pop into Reitmans." [It's exciting] to be part of something where you're throwing things on its head in a different way.'

Meghan was certainly the perfect model for the brand and as with so much in her life, she learned fast. Her mother had been a dressmaker and so becoming involved with the production aspect of it all harked back to her childhood. 'As I started to work with them, I was reminded that, growing up, my mom had all these little piecemeal jobs, one of which was her own little clothing line,' she continued. 'She made dresses, and I remember going with her to downtown LA to the fabric mart and visiting her pattern maker; she would sell these dresses on the side and I loved watching her do that. So launching this capsule collection of dresses feels serendipitous. This is something that I'm knowledgeable about and that I really enjoy.'

Meghan might have embraced this new and slightly less expensive style of dressing but the fact was she was still an actress and as such still had to attend red carpet events where she was totally on display and where the fashion pack and social media would have been on her back in an instant if she ever displayed less than perfect taste. One of the appealing aspects of her personality is that she is quite open about this, about the difficulties it presents and how frankly terrifying this could be. In doing so, it makes her seem closer to other aspirational young women – everyone knows what it is to worry about their looks.

'Red carpets are daunting,' she told *The Globe and*

Mail. 'I don't think they ever get comfortable, to be honest. I think that it's a very strange expectation, even though people assume that as an actor you would be comfortable modelling. Walking the red carpet is like being a model but the cameras are everywhere, so you don't even know exactly where to look and you can't protect your angle. And as women, we all have things that we're self-conscious about. I don't care how glamorous and perfect you think someone looks on the red carpet: I guarantee they're feeling nervous or insecure about some small thing. I think that's the part that's humanising. So, for me, what's very important is that we all support each other and empower each other, and say, take the risk. Feel good.'

The Reitmans association turned out to be beneficial in other ways too. By the time it came about Meghan had been living for much of the time in Canada for six years, and its success and the fact that she became part of a Canadian institution made her feel very much at home. The campaign was such that she regularly appeared on giant billboards, which was also bringing her to a whole new audience, one that might never even have seen *Suits*. It was, she acknowledged, making her feel very much at home. 'It's such an honour [to be a brand ambassador],' she said. 'It's super overwhelming. I don't think my parents fully understand what's happening up here because these billboards aren't in the States. For me, it's a huge moment especially because I feel like I've adopted Canada as much as it's adopted me in the past five years. This will be my sixth year living here, working on the show. And I'm here nine months out of the year. So I feel especially proud to be so connected to Reitmans, and to be embraced by Canada in a way that feels really special.'

The association turned out to be a great success, both for Meghan and Reitmans, which it seemed had indeed managed to be rejuvenated in the wake of their appointment of a sparkling new brand ambassador. It had turned out to be the perfect fit: the first collection sold massively well and there was a clear public demand for more.

Meghan now began to experience the pleasing but nonetheless difficult sensation of everyone wanting something from her. It was a sign of success, to be sure, but at the same time she risked burnout if she wasn't careful. She realised that just in time. 'Last year I learned the art of saying "no". Everyone tells you to strike when the iron's hot, which is hard not to get sucked into,' she told *Ebony* magazine, in February 2016. 'There comes a time when we need to say, "I have to take some time for me." I came to a point where I didn't feel like I had a moment to breathe, so I had to learn gradually to give myself some quietude. I love Russell Simmons's *Meditation Made Simple* app. It easily encourages you to quiet your mind. From a practical sense, I've learned to vacate on a plane, which is huge because I travel so much.'

In practice this involved a film, perhaps a glass of wine. 'It's the little things that feel like minutia, but at the end of the day, I can perform everything else so much better,' she added. 'At this point of my life, everything I'm doing I'm really passionate about. So even when it's exhausting, I still enjoy it because it's purpose driven. But I've also realised that if I didn't find that inner quiet, my inner peace, I might not be able to do it all. Now, at the end of a crazy day, I can sit down with a good friend, take a load off, breathe a sigh of relief, let go and begin anew.'

That said, there was more to come – much more. Meghan had put her public profile to good use commercially, but she was determined to do so in an ethical sense as well. She had been a campaigner since childhood: now this was to play a high profile in her adult life, too.

CHAPTER 7

THE CAMPAIGNER

Meghan has always been a campaigner. From early childhood she has taken up causes that concern her, and the forthright side of her nature meant she was never afraid to stand up for what she believed in. To a certain extent her personal circumstances motivated her: the issue of being a biracial woman had come up time and again throughout her life and she had never shied away from it, but that was by no means the only issue she was involved in. She remained concerned about many other issues into adulthood, something she had in common with Harry, who himself became a champion of the underdog and people with greater challenges in their lives – indeed, that was how they had met, through Harry's involvement with the Invictus Games.

Nor was it a surprise that he should be drawn to a woman who tried to make the world a better place – Harry's mother, Princess Diana, had been a great champion of the dispossessed, too. And it had always been touch and go as to whether Meghan would become an actress or do something seemingly 'worthier'. If, for whatever reason, an acting career became difficult to pursue, this was a very significant alternative string to her bow.

And so when Meghan realised that her profile was now such that she could turn it to good use, she did exactly that, taking on a number of causes and from 2014 onwards going public with her concerns in a much more high-profile way when the opportunities arose than previously. The first of these came in September that year when Meghan attracted some attention when she attended a UN Foundation hosted conference in Washington to discuss gender equality, a subject she was very keen to promote, and just the start of an ongoing relationship with the UN. Quite apart from anything else, she had now become a highly attractive commodity for such organisations: her growing profile meant that her very presence attracted increased attention to good causes.

This was just the start of it: later that year she attended the One Young World four-day conference in Dublin (a City Guide to Dublin subsequently appeared on The

Tig). One Young World is a UK-based organisation that invites young adults to address a selection of contemporary issues in the modern world, including them on panels with world leaders and information formers. It is widely considered to be extremely influential, with many high-profile supporters. One of Meghan's main concerns, both in this forum and elsewhere, was the subject of gender equality and to this end she took on the subject of nudity in music videos and on TV.

'In the show, for example, this season every script seemed to begin with Rachel entering wearing a towel and I said no, I'm not doing it anymore, I'm not doing it,' Meghan said in her speech. 'So I rang the creator and I was like, it's just gratuitous, we get it, we've already seen it once. So I think at a certain point you feel empowered enough to just say no. I think it's a challenging thing to do if you don't know your worth and your value for wanting to speak up. When you're an auditioning actress so hungry for work, of course you're willing do things like that. For me, speaking up and being able to say I'm not going to do that anymore has been a big shift for me personally. I only wish we had more time [at the conference]. It's amazing to see how empowered and passionate they are about these causes and this week the outcome is going to be incredible. More than anything I take away is I feel braver, I feel more energised and I feel we can really make something happen.'

She also addressed the issue of modern slavery: Meghan was partnered with one particular delegate, Luwam Estifanos, from Eritrea, who had been kept as a slave from the age of sixteen before she managed to run away and eventually ended up in Norway. She worked there as a campaigner to end slavery and she too addressed the conference.

From that moment on, Meghan kept up with her now high-profile commitments to good works – she was not one of those actresses who will occasionally show up to something to look good, but someone who takes an active and informed interest in her work. She became a UN Goodwill Ambassador and in August 2015 took part in a UN Public Service Award (PSA) in conjunction with KBS Toronto's Cause Company division in a Leaders PSA, designed to shed light on women with the potential to be leaders. Formally the UN Women's Advocate for Women's Leadership and Political Participation, and in a video shot for the campaign filled with young women looking as if they had potential, Meghan proclaimed, 'Today, less than one quarter of the world's leaders are women. We need more. Because when women lead, the world changes.' At that moment in the video, a light goes on over a young woman. 'We're working to create a world where women lead,' Meghan continued, coming back into the frame. 'Support us at UNWomen.org.'

This increasingly high-profile role came about not just because of Meghan's work on *Suits* but because of the initiatives she had made elsewhere too. 'It came about from what I did on The Tig: as well as food, travel, fashion, it was really trying to reshape the idea of beauty beyond the physical,' she told The Aesthete website. 'I write a lot of think pieces about women's empowerment or equality and I put them in the Beauty category. After I had written a piece on Independence Day about personal independence, I received an email from the Senior Advisor to the Executive Director of UN Women saying that they really liked what I was putting up, what I was using it for, and they wanted to work with me. I didn't believe it at first!'

She didn't just plunge in, however; Meghan conducted what would be called due diligence elsewhere. 'I wanted to see what they were doing at ground level,' she explained. 'It was important to not just attach my name to an organisation, even if it was the UN. I called and said, "I have a week off from filming, can I come work in the office for a week?" They replied that no one had ever asked that. I offered to fly myself there and back and work nine to five, and told them I wanted to shadow meetings and see what really happens. So I went to [UN Headquarters in] New York, every day in work attire, which is very funny because as an actress you don't have much suiting.' Indeed, she borrowed her clothes from the *Suits'* wardrobe.

It was the start of an entirely new aspect of her life. 'I went to morning briefings with the UN Secretary General's team and began understanding the pillars of the organisation so I knew where I wanted to invest my time,' she continued. 'As well as theatre, I studied International Relations at Northwestern and used to work for the US Embassy at Buenos Aires, which helped my decision to work on women's political participation and leadership. It's a space I feel comfortable in and am really excited about the future of, especially with the very strong possibility of Hillary putting her hat in the ring for office. [This interview was carried out before Hillary Clinton announced she would be running for President.] Once we realised that would be a comfortable fit for me, I went on a week's learning mission with the UN to Rwanda because it has the highest percentage of women in the parliamentary system of any country in the world. Sixty-four percent – unbelievable, given that twenty years ago they had their genocide. So I met female senators and went to a refugee camp to meet with women at the grassroots leadership level.' Rwanda was to become another recurring theme in Meghan's life and she was to visit the country when working for another charity as well.

Meghan drew on this experience when she gave a speech on International Woman's Day to UN Women 2015 in front of UN Secretary-General Ban Ki-moon, among many other notables, and got a standing ovation. 'Equality means that President Paul Kagame of Rwanda, whose country I recently visited as part of my learning mission with UN Women, is equal to the little girl in the Gihembe refugee camp, who is dreaming about being a president one day,' Meghan proclaimed in a passionate oration. 'Equality means that UN Secretary General Ban Ki-moon is equal to the young intern at the UN, who is dreaming about shaking his hand. It means a wife is equal to her husband, a sister to her brother. Not better nor worse – they are equal.'

She continued, 'As you all know, UN Women has defined the year 2030 as the expiration date for gender inequality. But studies show that at the current rate, the elimination of gender inequality will not be possible until 2095. That's another eighty years from now. And when it comes to women's political participation and leadership, the percentage of female parliamentarians globally has only increased by 11 per cent since 1995. Eleven per cent in twenty years?! This has to change... To have leaders such as President Kagame of Rwanda continue to be a role model of a country which has a parliamentary system comprised of 64 per cent female leaders! That's the highest of any government in the world. We need more men like that, just as we need more men like my father, who championed my eleven-year-old self to stand up for what is right. In doing this, we remind girls that their small voices are, in fact, not small, and that they can effect change. In doing this, we remind women that their involvement matters.'

Meghan had not come from a particularly privileged background and she had already seen a fair bit of the world, but Rwanda was a revelation in many different ways, opening up a world to her that she had not seen before. In an interview with *Destinations of the World News*, she said, 'I got to meet with the female senators as well as women working at a grass-roots level for leadership roles at Gihembe refugee camp, about two hours outside of Kigali. It was unbelievable. The work that I'm doing with the UN is so grounding in an industry where it's all first class and hair and makeup and glam; there's something really great about having a balance. I'm fortunate that

I grew up in this industry so I have a level head about it, but I do think that it's really nice to be able to have something that balances it all.'

In that, of course, she had a great deal in common with her future boyfriend. He too inhabited two vastly different worlds: that of royalty and that of his charity work. And while to be a Royal is not the same as being a celebrity there are certain obvious overlaps, and so Harry too went from enormous privilege to dealing with some of the poorest people in the world. Like Meghan, he developed a special association with Africa, not least through his charity Sentebale, founded to help children in the desperately poor country Lesotho, of which more anon.

Meghan made the provision of clean water another of her campaigns and linked up with World Vision to highlight the cause. She returned to Rwanda in early 2016, this time with World Vision to highlight the fact that young girls in particular were adversely affected by the need to walk for miles to get clean(ish) water. 'I don't sit around thinking about my titles and roles, I just do what feels right,' she told *Ebony*. 'They [World Vision] sent me the pitch. I did that gut check, and when I read the proposal – what they wanted to do in these communities in Rwanda – I had chills. How could I turn that down?

We have this life source that opens up such a sense of hope and creativity for these children, plus healthier lives for everyone in the community. It's amazing.'

The Watercolour Project was to build wells, which not only provided local communities with clean drinking water but also meant that young women would not have to undertake the long walks for water that had previously been their lot, and which as well as disrupting their schooling had opened them up to the risk of being trafficked. Meghan visited a school in the Gasabo region and taught the local children to paint with watercolours using water supplied by a newly installed local pipeline, before returning to Canada with the pictures in order to publicise the initiative.

'I had been familiar with World Vision from sponsoring a child in Malawi through the organisation over a decade ago,' she said in a statement to the artistcollective.ca. 'It's an organisation I respect and that I feel empowered to help effect change with. I was very fortunate to be able to visit with a community in Rwanda and teach them to paint with watercolours. It was impactful and beautiful to see them paint their dreams on paper. The contrast between communities that do and do not have access to clean water had a great impact on me. One borehole can bring life-giving water to as many as 500 people! I'm on a mission to build wells in Africa and I'm asking each of you to join me and see how many wells we can build together.'

This second visit to Rwanda had clearly made Meghan aware of the much wider issues and implications surrounding the topic of clean water: while an obvious necessity for a healthy life, it was related to far wider issues. 'I think there's a misconception that access to clean water is just about clean drinking water; which, of course, it is, but it's so much more than that,' she told Newswire. 'Access to clean water in a community keeps young girls in school, because they aren't walking hours each day to source water for their families. It allows women to invest in their own businesses and community. It promotes grassroots leadership, and, of course, it reinforces the health and wellness of children and adults. Every single piece of it is so interconnected, and clean water, this one life source, is the key to it all. It was an amazing experience, taking water from one of the water sources in the community and using it with the children to paint pictures of what they dream to be when they grow up. I saw that water is not just a life source for a community, but it can really be a source for creative imagination, and how lucky I am to have been a part of that.'

In 2016, Meghan again appeared at a One Young World Summit, this time held closer to home, in Ottawa. Canada's charismatic Prime Minister Justin Trudeau was on hand to help matters kick off: 'What you do, what you say, and the choices you make have the power to change the world,' he told attendees, who also included Emma Watson, Sir Bob Geldof, former UN Secretary-General Kofi Annan, nobel laureate Muhammad Yunus, Oscar-winning producer Jon Landau, Cher and Bruce Dickinson of Iron Maiden.

The close of the year saw another campaign, again on the subject of women's issues: Meghan became one of a number of high-profile signatories to an open letter organised by the ONE campaign as part of its Poverty is Sexist initiative, calling for an education for millions of girls suffering from poverty. Fellow signees included Facebook COO Sheryl Sandberg, YouTube CEO Susan Wojcicki, actresses Charlize Theron and Blake Lively, and musicians Bob Geldof and Lady Gaga.

Meghan also put the campaign's statement out on Twitter. Now firmly ensconced with Harry, she was aware that her profile was higher – and as such people followed everything she did much more closely than previously. Her support for good causes was becoming more sought after than ever.

She was aware that she was now moving in two completely different worlds and in her article for *Elle* said that although it was possible to balance the two, it did rather hit home when she was making her way back from Rwanda to Canada and received an email from her manager asking if she could attend the Baftas. 'And in that moment, my gut said no because while my two worlds can co-exist, I've learned that being able to keep a foot in both is a delicate balance,' she wrote. 'No, they are not mutually exclusive but guiding my heart through the swinging pendulum from Hollywood fantasy to third-world reality is challenging in its own way… While my life shifts from refugee camps to red carpets, I choose them both because these worlds can, in fact, co-exist. And for me, they must.'

Those worlds co-existed for her future boyfriend, too. While on the surface Meghan and Harry might not have seemed to have a great deal in common, to look at either of their lives is to see that both have high-profile roles in a world of grandeur and privilege and yet both have chosen to use their profile not only to do some good in the world but also to do some good in the same part of the world – Africa. And although their childhoods were very different, both know the pain of parents divorcing, both have experienced failed relationships and both have overcome early obstacles when finding their way in the world. In fact, the closer you look, the more obvious it is that they are the perfect match.

CHAPTER 8

AN HEIR AND A SPARE

I t was on 15 September 1984 that Princess Diana gave birth to her second son with Prince Charles: Henry Charles Albert David made his way into the world at St Mary's Hospital in Paddington, London, as had his older brother William before him, and indeed William's own two children would do three decades hence. Although his parents' marriage still ostensibly appeared to be happy to the public, at home it was a different matter and the union was already crumbling. Harry was to spend his early years in what became known as the 'War of the Waleses'.

None of this was known to the wider world. In the early years of the Waleses' marriage, the public image of the most scrutinised relationship of the day was totally at odds with the private reality. When Lady Diana Spencer, the third surviving child of John, later Earl, Spencer and his wife, Frances, married Prince Charles on 29 July 1981, the world fell in love with the shy young aristocrat, blushing behind her pie-crust collars, and watched, open-mouthed, as she metamorphosed into the most photogenic icon of the 1980s and beyond.

Diana was just twenty when they married and Charles thirty-two; it soon emerged that there were problems from the beginning. He loved the country life, and Diana turned out to be an aficionado of the town. Charles enjoyed serious music; Diana, in those long ago days of the early 1980s, was given the name (that she disliked) 'Disco Di'. Charles enjoyed classical literature; Diana's tastes leaned more towards the blockbuster romance. And so it went on. The 'suitable, attractive, and sweet-charactered girl' proved herself to be quite the handful for the then-traditional Royal family. Charles clearly had no idea how to cope and worst of all the public's obsession with Diana showed no sign of abating. Charles, who had been brought up as a future monarch and was used to being the centre of attention, found himself for the first time in his life playing second fiddle.

Despite all this, however, the couple managed to

Above left: Prince Harry greets a young fan on the final day of the Invictus Games in Orlando, Florida, May 2016. It is here that the couple supposedly met.

(© Chris Jackson/Getty Images for Invictus)

Above right: Presenting a medallion to a member of the Invictus Games GB team.

(© GREGG NEWTON/AFP/Getty Images)

Below left: Harry in his military regalia, attending the Armistice Day service at the National Memorial Arboretum on November 11, 2016.

(© Mark Cuthbert/UK Press via Getty Images)

Below right: Discussing tactics with England Rugby player James Haskell during an England rugby squad training session at Twickenham for the RBS Six Nations Championship, February 2017.

(© Kirsty Wigglesworth - WPA Pool/Getty Images)

Above: Both heavily involved in philanthropy and charity work, here Prince Harry is in Newcastle, talking to runners for the charity Heads Together during their training for the 2016 London Marathon.

Below: Meghan Markle taking part in a Q&A at the Reebok Women's #HonorYourDays event in 2016.

(© Darren McCollester/Getty Images for REEBOK)

Above: Meghan Markle starring in Season Six of TV drama *Suits* as Rachel Zane, the role that made her famous.

(© Shane Mahood/USA Network/ NBCU Photo Bank via Getty Images)

Left: Harry and Meghan seen together for the first time at an official engagement, at the Invictus Games in Toronto, September 2017.

Prince Harry and Meghan Markle, on the announcement of their engagement in the Sunken Garden at Kensington Palace on 27th November 2017.

(© Chris Jackson/Getty Images)

maintain some semblance of normality, in public at least. After a wedding that was watched on television by 750 million people worldwide (and in which Diana called her groom Philip Charles Arthur George instead of Charles Philip, a portent, some felt, of chaos to come), the couple moved into Kensington Palace and Highgrove House near Tetbury in Gloucestershire, the two locations that were to be Harry's childhood homes. Diana's first pregnancy was announced in November 1981; some years later it emerged that in January 1982 she had fallen down a staircase at Sandringham. The Royal Gynaecologist Sir George Pinker examined her and although the Princess had hurt herself, the baby was untouched. William Arthur Philip Louis was born on 21 June 1982. The fact that the Royal couple intended to follow a very different style of parenting was evidenced when they took him on a major tour of Australia and New Zealand. The Queen and Prince Philip had left Charles at home when they undertook tours in his early childhood; such were the feelings about such a change of direction that eyebrows were raised.

The joke in aristocratic circles is that there is always the need for an 'heir and a spare' to provide back-up in case the heir should have some kind of accident. The Queen herself produced not one spare but three. And so in due course Diana fell pregnant again, a period which she later said was the happiest in her marriage and so it was ironic that after Harry was born the relationship with her husband began to fall apart for good. Many extremely negative stories were bandied about by the press at the time; a particularly scandalous accusation was that Charles was not Harry's biological father at all. That honour was accorded to Diana's later lover, the undeniably red-haired James Hewitt. However, it has been widely accepted that the affair with Hewitt began in 1986, two years after Harry's birth, and it is also possible to state pretty accurately that around the time of Harry's conception at the end of 1983, the Royals celebrated Christmas at Windsor Castle and Sandringham, making it highly unlikely that James Hewitt was snooping around the Palace corridors. Furthermore, the person Harry genuinely most resembles is his maternal Aunt Sarah, while pictures of him as a young child hark back to those of his paternal grandfather, the Duke of Edinburgh.

'What we saw after the birth of Harry was a lot of speculation and rumour that Harry was the son of James Hewitt,' Ken Wharfe – Diana's sometime bodyguard, who has written a great deal about his time with the Princess – told the documentary makers behind *Harry: The Mysterious Prince*. 'Statistically, we know that was impossible. I know personally it wasn't because the Princess told me so and I think really that's where the matter ends.'

The journalist Richard Kay, a friend and confidante of Diana during her lifetime, also appeared in the documentary: 'There are some physical characteristics that I will commend to you: Harry, his brother, his father, and his grandfather, Prince Philip, share one thing in common – they all have sausage fingers!' he said. But Harry's arrival did undoubtedly coincide with a froideur in his parents' relationship that was soon to descend into outright war.

Right from the start the young Henry was known as Harry. Baptised on 21 December 1984 at St George's Chapel, Windsor Castle, by the then Archbishop of Canterbury, Robert Runcie, who had also officiated at his parents' wedding ceremony, Harry's education and childhood was to be very different from that of his father; it was a far more liberal upbringing in many ways, but of course with all the trauma that was to come played out in the public eye. Like his elder brother, to whom he was very close right from the start, Harry was introduced to Royal tours early, when his parents took him along to Italy in 1985. As previously mentioned, Prince Charles had been left behind when his own parents carried out their Royal duties and neither he nor Diana wanted to replicate that.

It is a widely accepted fact that in the birth order of children, the elder one tends to be more establishment and conservative, the younger more rebellious and wild. So it was with William and Harry. Diana would refer to her younger son as 'Your Royal Naughtiness'. In letters addressed to the late Cyril Dickman, a Buckingham Palace steward, that came to light in October 2016, an early missive bears witness to the strong bond between the brothers, noting William was 'swamping Harry with an endless supply of hugs and kisses, hardly letting the parents near'. A later letter, dated 18 July 1993, notes, 'The boys are well and enjoying boarding school a lot, although Harry is constantly in trouble'. It was to be a theme that continued throughout his life.

The travails of their early life established a bond between William and Harry that was to endure. On the one hand the brothers grew up in the lap of privilege, commuting between Kensington Palace in London and Highgrove in Gloucestershire, attending the best schools, travelling the world from a young age, mixing in aristocratic circles and learning that their destiny was to move among the great and the good, the elite to whom so much was given. And yet, at the same time, they were in a goldfish bowl; their mother was the most photographed woman in the world.

This was something she had extremely ambivalent feelings about, for Diana cultivated the press. She had known favourites among journalists and comments from 'friends of Diana' were known to have come from the Princess herself. On the other hand, as interest in her grew and intensified during her lifetime, it became evident that by encouraging the media to take an interest in her, she had unleashed a force she could not contain. The attention could not be turned off when she wanted privacy. The boys saw all this and more. What they also witnessed at first hand, of course, was the increasingly terrible relationship between Charles and Diana. Their powerlessness to escape the tension between their parents, combined with a growing mistrust of the media that they thought hounded their mother, drew them closer together, establishing the extremely close bond that endures to this day.

Harry's education was to follow a precedent set down by his mother's side of the family, not his father's, not least as Charles complained very publicly about how much he had hated his own school days at the remote and austere Scottish institution Gordonstoun. Harry's first outing was to Jane Mynors nursery school in London's Notting Hill Gate, an early sign that his mother was going to attempt to at least show him what a normal life looked like, before he became entirely swamped in Royal privilege. However, there were reports that he was bullied by other children: even at the age of three, Harry was set apart from his peers by merit of being a member of the Royal family. The other children knew there was something different about him and took it out on him. Harry's sunny nature as an adult is all the more remarkable given that he had to put up with a lot while still so young.

After that, from the age of four he attended the pre-preparatory Wetherby School in London, starting a week late due to illness and famously pictured on his first day shaking hands with the headmistress. Wetherby, with its uniform of grey blazer piped in red, had a reputation for being one of the fiercer pre-prep schools: its pupils came from wealthy families who wanted only the best for their offspring, who tended to end up at the country's top public schools. Both boys were pictured at the start of each term, Harry clutching his Bugs Bunny satchel, sometimes smiling for the cameras and sometimes being encouraged to behave by his mother, who always accompanied the boys.

Harry then followed in the footsteps of William and

went on to Ludgrove School. This was a well-regarded independent boarding school based in Berkshire with a reputation for sending its pupils on to some of the most prestigious schools in the country, but Harry's arrival coincided with one of the worst periods of his parents' marriage, leading to fears that he might be bullied on the back of it. Rumours of their problems had now become public, but in 1992, matters went far beyond fiction as the mighty House of Windsor began to resemble nothing so much as a luridly written soap.

In May that year the book *Diana: Her True Story* by Andrew Morton appeared in the bookshops and was an immediate sensation. Although the extent of Diana's involvement did not become clear until after her death, it was clear right from the start that she had at the very least given friends tacit encouragement to speak on her behalf (in fact, she had contributed directly, as later became clear). The book laid clear the full disaster ground that the Royal marriage had become, detailing the affair between Charles and Camilla Parker-Bowles and even Diana's bulimia and suicide attempts. It caused furore and was in part responsible for the couple's eventual separation and divorce.

Nineteen ninety-two, which the Queen was later to describe as her 'annus horribilis', just grew worse and worse. In August, tapes surfaced of Diana talking on the phone to one of her lovers, James Gilbey, a Lotus car-dealer and heir to the gin fortune of the same name. The two were obviously extremely intimate, with James repeatedly calling Diana 'darling' and 'squidgy'.

There was a great deal more of this – as well as intimate details of the inner workings and relationships of the Royal family – and the media coverage of it was non-stop, bordering on the hysterical. It emerged that the tape had been made a couple of years earlier on New Year's Eve 1989; there were numerous theories about how it eventually got into the public domain (and no completely satisfactory version of events has ever been established) with speculation that Charles's camp had released the tapes in revenge for the Morton book. If so, the Prince didn't have to wait long for a similar embarrassment; another newspaper broke the story of the Camillagate tapes, in which Charles and his lover, Camilla Parker-Bowles were heard engaging in equally intimate chat. Worse, still, Charles was heard joking in very explicit fashion with his lady friend; this tape, too, appeared to have been recorded several years previously, before 'Squidgygate'. Again, no one was sure how it got into the public domain. And then, in the background, there were further disasters: the Duke and Duchess of York split up, Windsor Castle burnt down and finally, the separation of the Prince and Princess of Wales was announced.

All this and more could not have been more public and although William and Harry's schools tried to protect them, a certain amount of gossip was bound to get out. And as Charles and Diana grew increasingly estranged, both seeking solace elsewhere, they began providing two different versions of childhood for their sons. When they were with Diana, the boys were dressed in jeans and trainers and were taken on outings to fast-food restaurants and amusement parks, again in an attempt to show them the way most people lived. Back at home they were introduced to charity work, especially concerning the homeless and AIDS, which at the time was widely considered a shocking subject for a member of the Royal family to be involved with. Indeed, Princess Diana even visited Bosnia and Herzegovina as part of her campaign to ban landmines and also walked through an active minefield in Angola – a ground-breaking feat that would never be allowed to happen now, and one that showed the Princess in her true light among the awful accusations and press intrusion that surrounded her. The Princess, in fact, became a leading light in the battle against AIDS (famously holding hands with a dying AIDS patient), and was one of the people directly responsible for de-stigmatising the deadly disease.

Under the supervision of Charles, however, the boys usually appeared far more formally attired, with jacket and tie, taking part in typically Royal pastimes such as riding and hunting, which Harry grew to love. By now, Prince Charles had moved out of Kensington Palace to make St James's Palace his London base, but Highgrove remained his real home. Harry had a floppy-eared rabbit at Highgrove that he kept as a pet and fed with carrots he grew himself. He learned to shoot, which he also loved: he once accidentally shot a moorhen on his father's pond – but gained brownie points in the eyes of Charles by owning up to what he had done. The boys were also given a mini-Aston Martin, an exact replica of their father's car, which they would motor around the estate.

However, the separation did nothing to calm matters between the warring Prince and Princess of Wales; if anything, it did the opposite. And in 1994, Charles merely compounded matters by appearing in a television interview with Jonathan Dimbleby in which he admitted his relationship with Camilla. Things finally came to a head when Diana appeared on an episode of the current affairs programme *Panorama* on the BBC in November 1995. And when the programme aired, it revealed publicly for the first time the full extent of the anger and bitterness that had been brewing. Diana questioned

Charles's fitness to be King, spoke of her enemies at the Palace, admitted to a relationship with James Hewitt, informed the world that 'there were three of us in the marriage, so it was a bit crowded' and added that she did not expect to become Queen but wanted instead to be the 'Queen of People's Hearts'.

Such a situation could not be allowed to continue, and it proved so: the Queen wrote to Charles and Diana telling them they must divorce. And so the institution of monarchy, which had been so rocked by a divorcee just six decades earlier, found itself rocked to the core once again by a divorce. Lengthy negotiations began, which ended with Diana receiving a lump sum of £17 million plus £400,000 a year, but the loss of her HRH title. That HRH was the cause of some controversy: according to Tina Brown's biography of Diana, *The Diana Chronicles*, her father-in-law, Prince Philip, had told her, 'If you don't behave, my girl, we'll take away your title.' 'My title [Lady Diana Spencer] is a lot older than yours, Philip,' Diana replied. William, just fourteen at the time, apparently stepped in and told his mother that he, William, would restore the title when he acceded to the throne.

After the separation had been formalised, the boys' father took on staff to help him when he had custody of his sons, most notably a former nursery teacher called

Alexandra 'Tiggy' Legge-Bourke, daughter of the late William and Shân Legge-Bourke, lady-in-waiting to the Princess Royal. Tiggy, an outdoorsy type who had grown up on the Glanusk Estate in South Wales, joined the household in 1993 and William and Harry adored her. She was to play an important part in their lives, a relationship that remains to this day. However, particularly in Diana's eyes, Tiggy made several mistakes: she referred to the boys as 'my babies', which sent Diana's hackles through the roof, and then managed to make matters worse by somewhat rudely comparing her parenting style with that of Diana's. 'I give them what they need… fresh air, a rifle and a horse,' she said. 'She gives them a tennis racket and a bucket of popcorn at the movies.'

Diana, understandably, was enraged. As the divorce negotiations went on, the Princess reportedly started a rumour that Tiggy was having an affair with Charles; worse, she insinuated that a recent minor operation had in fact been an abortion. Matters came to a head at a staff Christmas party: instructing a fellow guest to watch her, Diana was said to have marched straight up to Tiggy and announced, 'So sorry to hear about the baby.' Tiggy fled the room in tears and her parents actually threatened legal action on her behalf before frantic behind-the-scenes activity manged to calm the matter down.

Meanwhile, there were other traumas to endure. As Harry prepared to follow William to Eton, Prince Charles had to have a talk with him, in which he warned him that there was gossip that James Hewitt was actually his real father. Charles assured him that this was not the case, but even having to listen to such a thing must have been torture for a young child. And then came the loss that was to mark him for life – that of his beloved mother.

CHAPTER 9

CHILDHOOD'S
END

When the world woke up on the morning of Sunday, 31 August 1997 to the news that Diana, Princess of Wales, had been killed in a car crash in the Pont de l'Alma tunnel in Paris with her boyfriend, Dodi Fayed, the sense of shock was so profound that to many millions around the world it was as if they had lost a member of their own family. Diana had been simply everywhere that summer, namely on front pages on an almost daily basis all over the world. The divorce from Prince Charles had come through in August 1996, which meant that for the first time Princess Diana could openly have another man in her life: at the time of her death that man had been Dodi Fayed, son of the Egyptian billionaire Mohamed Al-Fayed.

All summer Diana had been in the news, from the charity auction of some of her dresses in June to a series of summer holidays, both with and without Dodi. There had been another high-profile trip, to Bosnia and Herzegovina as part of her campaign to ban landmines, and mounting speculation that she and Dodi were to get engaged or that Diana was pregnant – or that the Royal family was concerned about the relationship – that had created a frenzy around her. Even by the usual standards of Diana-mania, that summer had been a complete circus. She was spotted posing on yachts, and, in a last haunting shot, was seen leaving the Ritz hotel in Paris and peering behind her at the assembled paparazzi, as the car that would take her to her death sped off.

Amid all the shock and recrimination that followed her tragic death, as an ocean of flowers grew outside Kensington Palace and the mood of the populace threatened to turn ugly, it was easy to forget that there were two small boys that no longer had a mother. And as millions who had never met her claimed they were inconsolable in their grief, the ground had fallen out from beneath William and Harry's feet. They had been holidaying with their mother earlier in the summer but were with their father and grandparents in the Royal family's Scottish retreat Balmoral when the dreadful news came through. Prince Charles was forced to break the news to his sons before the assembled Royals, brought up to put duty first and wear the mask of the stiff upper lip, went en masse to church. Harry, unable to take in the magnitude of what had happened, was said to have asked, 'Is Mummy really dead?'

The Windsors were to come in for some severe criticism in the wake of Diana's death, much of it devoted to their behaviour towards the two boys. Indeed, the Royals next came in for such negative comment that a whiff of republicanism seemed to be entering the national debate. Diana had been an astronomically popular figure and there was an enormous amount of sympathy for her among the British public, who felt she had been very harshly treated by a Royal family who had used her for breeding purposes and then expected her to toe the line.

But that was by no means the full picture: Diana was a very complicated woman and quite as capable of fighting her own corner as anyone. Irrespectively, the public loved her and they had lost her, and the refusal of the Royals to return to London and join in the nation's grief was turning the public mood ugly. 'Ma'am, show us you care,' the newspapers cried as another row blew up, this time over whether the flag over Buckingham Palace should be flown at half mast. This was not protocol and had not even been done for the Queen Mother, but such was the strength of feeling that protocol was done away with – and the flag flew halfway down the pole.

One of the reasons the Royal family had stayed in Scotland was to do exactly what the public was urging them to do: look after the boys. As the shock and grief sank in, William and Harry were to some extent protected away from the grieving crowds, but it was now plain that if they didn't return to the capital, there would be a real emergency on the Establishment's hands. And so the first the public saw of twelve-year-old Harry, the little boy who had lost his mum, was when he emerged, holding tightly on to Prince Charles's hand, to inspect the flowers that seemed at times to be coating the whole of the centre of London. It was a heartbreaking sight and it created a sense of loss in both brothers that could never go away.

Diana's funeral took place a week later, on 6 September. Although it was a hugely public event, watched by 2 billion people around the world, again it was brought home to the public that at the centre of it were two children who had lost their mum. When the coffin first came into view, it had three wreaths of flowers adorning it, including one marked 'Mummy'. Diana's body was taken in a funeral cortège from Kensington Palace to St James's Palace, where Prince Philip, Prince Charles, Diana's brother Earl Spencer, William and Harry joined it and walked behind the gun carriage carrying the coffin all the way to Westminster Abbey. In this they were encouraged by Prince Philip, who had not in fact initially planned to walk himself, but learned that his grandsons were feeling unsure. 'If I walk, will you walk with me?' he asked William and so the two boys accompanied their mother on her way.

Two thousand mourners attended the funeral, including former British prime ministers Margaret Thatcher, James Callaghan and Edward Heath, and former Conservative MP Winston Churchill, the grandson of World War II-era Prime Minister Sir Winston Churchill. Others included Sir Cliff Richard, Hillary Clinton, Henry Kissinger, William J. Crowe, Bernadette Chirac, Queen Noor of Jordan, Tom Hanks, Steven Spielberg, Elton John, George Michael, Michael Barrymore, Mariah Carey, Richard Branson, Luciano Pavarotti, Tom Cruise and Nicole Kidman, reflecting the true breadth of Diana's influence in the world. The then Prime Minister Tony Blair read an excerpt from the First Epistle to the Corinthians: 'And now abideth faith, hope, love, these three; but the greatest of these is love.'

The boys had always been close; this just brought them closer. To be at the centre of such a maelstrom with only each other to rely on drew them together and that autumn, now thirteen, Harry followed his older brother to Eton. It was the first time he had started a new school without Diana to look after him, but Charles was by his side. The two posed for pictures, with Harry managing to smile for the assembled photographers, before entering Manor House, where he was to board in the same house as William, now sixteen.

The next few years were to be spent in the company of the cream of Britain's educational elite: Harry, like all Etonians, would have his own maid (and, unlike all Etonians, his own bodyguard, who slept in the next room), and would wear the uniform of black tailcoat, waistcoat and stiff collar. He was not as academic as William and so there had been concerns that Eton might be too much for him, but because his birthday was in September, he had been able to spend another year at Ludgrove. He managed to pass the Common Entrance Exam and was known to want to be at the same school as William. Another advantage to Eton was that it is very close to Windsor Castle, where his grandparents spent many weekends.

Eton was generally accepted as being the best place

to educate the great and the good and not just in the UK. Founded by Henry VI, it has been the alma mater to nineteen British prime ministers, including David Cameron, and lists George Orwell, Henry Fielding, Aldous Huxley, Percy Shelley and Ian Fleming among its alumni. More recently it has also produced a number of top calibre actors, including Eddie Redmayne, who was a contemporary of Prince William. There is a language singular to Etonians which outsiders don't always understand: cricketers are known as 'dry bobs', rowers as 'wet bobs', while 'slack bobs' do neither. Lessons are 'schools' – 'divs' to the boys – and teachers are 'beaks'. There is a huge amount of extra-curricular activity on offer, everything from astronomy to country dancing, and Eton is also the home of the Eton Wall Game. This is a form of football in which it is very difficult to score – although Harry did.

But Harry never did improve academically. He excelled at sports, especially polo, skiing and shooting, all activities his family encouraged in his spare time, and while at Eton he joined the Combined Cadet Force (aka the Eton Rifles), the first sign that he might be interested in a military career. Behind the scenes, however, he started to develop the characteristics of a bad boy: he'd reportedly first puffed on a cigarette aged eight and had tried alcohol aged twelve. He got a little too fond of it: Charles was hugely embarrassed when, during his fiftieth birthday party, Harry stripped off and ran naked among the guests. (Similar antics were going to get him into trouble at a later stage too.)

One problem was that with Diana gone, Charles was acutely aware that the boys had no mother and he tried to overcompensate. He also wasn't around that much, having his own Royal duties to fulfil. That meant he didn't keep as close an eye on his youngest son as he could have done, not least when Harry would invite friends home to Highgrove during the summer holidays and entertain them in the cellar of the house, a place he called Club H. Harry began dabbling in drugs when the far more sober and sensible William was away on a gap year; it is thought that it began when he started visiting a pub called the Rattlebone in nearby Sherston and met a group of slightly older friends, including Guy Pelly.

At Eton he was known as 'Hash Harry' and when a policeman found him stoned at a pub, Prince Charles was informed. The shocked Prince sent his son to a rehabilitation unit for drug users – the sort of action Princess Diana might have taken – in order for him to see for himself the damage drugs could do. 'The Prince talked to Harry and he admitted it straight away,' a friend told the *Daily Mail* in 2002. 'There was no point in screaming and shouting at him. The Prince is a patron of a number of drugs charities and he took advice from the experts. He decided it would be a good idea for Harry to spend a day talking to people coming out of cocaine and heroin addiction to see what happens to you if you start taking drugs. He wants Harry to learn from hard experience. These are hard heroin addicts and consequences of their drug abuse shocked Harry into realising what he was doing was not the right path to go down and that the people he was mixing with were not the right friends to have.'

It was a wake-up call not just for Harry but for others around him who realised that he was still extremely young and impressionable and needed a sobering influence. He was also beginning to attract a fair bit of female attention. Harry was at an age when girls were going to play a part in his life.

'There have been some wild times with Harry here,' Rattlebone regular David Bragg told the *News of the World*. 'You ask anyone around here. Unless they're being very loyal they'll agree. He came here quite often. Of course a lot of young girls from villages round here would come to try and catch his eye. You can hardly blame them, can you? I've seen him crawl out of barns here covered in straw, brushing his hair. Harry's been the worse for wear and pretty crazy, he certainly liked a drink, and there's been some dancing on tables and chatting up girls. On one occasion I remember he was on TV waving to the crowds from Buckingham Palace and a few hours later he was here in the pub with us.'

Once two teenage sisters enlisted David's help in persuading their mother to let them visit Club H. 'I went to their mother and said, "Look, you must trust them and let them go because they may never get another chance to go to Highgrove,"' he said. 'Two of the girls who've just left [the pub when the reporter was present] were in the papers with Harry. They were messing around, ruffling his hair. He got hold of one of them, called Emma Lippiatt, and picked her up. She put her legs around him, and he swung her around. They were just being coltish.'

The pictures appeared in the press. Farmer's daughter Emma Lippiatt was one of Harry's earliest girlfriends, two years older than him and a so-called member of the 'glosse posse'. She had nothing to do with his drug taking and the couple were to stay together until he met Chelsy Davy.

But Harry was still at school and there were growing rumours that he was if anything less academically inclined than previously thought. His GCSE results were never released to the public and in later years he confirmed what everyone had suspected – that he had not been that happy at school. 'I didn't enjoy school at all,' he told teenagers at the Ottery Centre in Cape Town, which worked to rehabilitate gang leaders. 'I would like to have come to a place like this. When I was at school I wanted to be the bad boy.' Harry was far from being the only prince who wanted that, but at that point he was third in line to the throne, a position he was well aware of. He was also a bereaved youngster and as such, vulnerable in ways that his bravado could not entirely conceal. That he had a considerably more thoughtful side was also evident, as shown when he went to visit his former nanny, Tiggy Legge-Bourke, who was now married and had given birth to her first child: Harry went to visit her two weeks after the baby was born and took the child out for a spin in the fresh air to give his mother a break.

Harry's reputation as a party prince stayed with him throughout his teens. Some holidays would be spent at the Cornwall resort of Rock, which, somewhat to its residents' displeasure, gained a reputation as a summer destination young Sloanes would go to misbehave. There continued to be reports of drunkenness and partying, but far from turning the public against Harry, many responded with sympathy on the grounds that, after all, he had lost his mother. There was a sense of a young man adrift, without the guidance he needed. Prince William had left Eton to go first on a gap year and then on to the University of St Andrews in northern Scotland, far away from Eton.

Harry, even in his teens, was becoming quite the man about town: he was spotted at polo matches and at one point was seen with the German supermodel Claudia Schiffer. Holidays were taken to Spanish resorts such as Marbella and Sotogrande, where his protection officers made sure that any high jinks stayed strictly private. But there did need to be some thought about his future and Harry had by now decided he definitely wanted to join the military, which meant a stint at Sandhurst. However, that in turn meant that he needed two A-levels and there was some doubt as to whether he would achieve that.

In the end he did, although that too was not without controversy. Harry managed to get a grade B in art and a D in geography, enough to get him to Sandhurst, but the achievement was overshadowed by claims that a teacher had helped him to cheat. Both Harry and Eton denied the allegations, which came about after his former art teacher Sarah Forsyth, brought a claim of wrongful dismissal against the school: she related that the night before a moderator was due to visit the school to look at the students' AS level work, Ian Burke, head of art, asked her to prepare some words to go with Harry's Expressive Project, in which the student must explain his own work and relate it to one of the great artists. In a rather nasty case, in which the teacher admitted to taping Harry saying he only wrote 'about a sentence' of his work, with claims of drinking and bullying by another teacher and aspersions about her own mental stability, she further asserted that it was widely accepted that Harry was not the academic type, as well as saying that Ian contributed to some of Harry's artwork which, embarrassingly, had ended up in a newspaper. In the event, she won her claim for wrongful dismissal, but the exam board cleared Harry of cheating.

It was his first taste of the somewhat negative press he was to receive in the wake of some ill-advised future activities and he sounded resigned: 'Maybe [the accusations] it's just part of who I am,' he said. 'I have to deal with it. There's lots of things people get accused of. Unfortunately mine are public.'

The allegations didn't become public immediately, and before Harry enrolled at Sandhurst, it was decided that he should take a gap year, which would be the first time he travelled abroad without his father. Many teenagers take gap years, of course, but in the case of the Royals it is deemed to be a particularly beneficial activity, because it gives them a chance to spend time in environs that are not as cushy as the ones in which they grew up; it also gives them the chance to see a bit of the world before knuckling down to full-time Royal duty.

His first destination was Australia (which prompted complaints about the £600,000 security bill), where he went to work as a 'jackaroo' or farm hand on the 39,500-acre Tooloombilla station in the outback near Roma, in central Queensland. His presence prompted such strong media interest that there were initial reports he would leave, but Harry was having none of it. He loved it; working from 7am to 6pm in the open air was far more to his taste than a study or classroom. The station was owned by old friends of his mother, Annie and Noel Hill, and Harry learned how to handle cattle, repair damaged fencing and general farm maintenance. In his spare time he watched the rugby: 'I have had a great time working out here, meeting people and learning a bit about how to be a jackeroo and, of course, the rugby was absolutely fantastic,' he said. 'It's a great country.'

Against a background of yet more drama, in this case his mother's former butler, Paul Burrell, publishing a book about Diana ('Cold and overt betrayal,' said both princes in a statement, 'abusing his position'), Harry spent three months on the ranch, clearly loving every minute of it and completely disabusing doubters who had publicly said he would spend his time in Oz playing polo. He was pictured out on a horse called Guardsman, completely in control and playing his own part on the ranch.

But it was what he did next that was an indication that Harry was far more than just another rich boy out to have fun. As already discussed, his mother had been a passionate advocate of AIDS charities and in a clear sign that he wanted to carry on her work, Harry visited the tiny African country of Lesotho. While present in the little-known kingdom in the mountains, he visited an orphanage for children with AIDS, and helped to build a clinic and road bridge. The experience had a big impact on him. The journalist Tom Bradby accompanied him: 'His bond with so many of the orphans whose lives had been blighted by HIV and Aids appeared heartfelt,' he told the *Radio Times*. 'The connection with his mother and her work was there for all to see and when I asked him about her – well, a whole lot of emotion came tumbling out. He was a bruised young man with a lot to say.'

And a lot to do. Harry did not forget his time in Lesotho and once back in the UK established his charity, Sentebale ('forget me not'), to carry on the work. Much like his mother, he had proved he had both a fun-loving and a serious side. And while his immediate future was the Army, good works were what he wanted to do in the longer term.

CHAPTER 10

MILITARY MAN

On 8 May 2005, Harry entered the Royal Military Academy Sandhurst as Officer Cadet Wales and joined the Alamein Company, the start of what was to prove an impressive military career. Harry might not have been particularly academic but he was to master the art of handling some complex machinery during his time in the army, very much proving wrong the doubters who dismissed him as a lightweight. To get in, he had had to pass a four-day Royal Commissions Board assessment, which was no picnic: he had to tackle an assault course, complete fitness tests including fifty sit-ups and forty-four press-ups in two minutes, complete written tasks about how he would tackle emergencies, and compete in races. Harry passed but had to delay his entry from January to May due to a knee injury sustained while training with the Army ahead of his test, which was made worse when coaching a group of children for the Rugby Football Union.

There is a long tradition of military service within the Royal family. Prince William served within several branches, including the Navy and the RAF; Prince Charles served in the Navy and the RAF; Prince Andrew had quite a distinguished career in the forces and fought in the Falklands; Prince Philip would almost certainly have risen to the top of the Royal Navy had his wife not become the British Head of State several decades earlier than expected; even Prince Edward had a short stint in the Royal Marines before deciding that military life was not for him.

A time with the military was generally felt to be beneficial for a member of the Royal family for a variety of reasons: for a start, there was the element of serving your country; secondly, it provided a career that could not possibly be said to have been dependent on Royal connections and, of course, it gave the relevant individual some focus in life. For the direct heirs to the throne who will one day get the top job, including Prince Charles, Prince William and also Prince George, military service is seen as part of a good training for the role but not the be-all and end-all. For others, such as Harry, who would have to find a focus for their life, it has the potential to provide a long-term and worthwhile career.

And Harry needed a focus in his life, to say nothing of making amends for some spectacularly stupid and offensive behaviour earlier in the year. He was getting a reputation for rowdy behaviour, having had a skirmish with a photographer at a nightclub, and then worse – far worse – pictures had circulated of him at a fancy dress party with the theme 'colonial and native'. Harry, by now twenty, turned up wearing a German desert uniform with a swastika armband, leading to the almost inevitable headline 'Harry The Nazi'. He could hardly have chosen a more odious costume and the moment the pictures emerged realised this straight away.

A statement was rushed out: 'Prince Harry has apologised for any offence or embarrassment he has caused. He realises it was a poor choice of costume,' it said. But this was not so lightly shrugged off: there were calls for Harry to make an apology in person rather than through a statesman, not least from the then Conservative leader Michael Howard, who was Jewish, while a Labour MP claimed it showed he was not fit to attend Sandhurst. The Board of Deputies of British Jews and the then Reform Synagogues of Great Britain took a considerably more emollient approach, however, in both cases observing that it was in bad taste, but that Harry had apologised and the apology should be accepted. That incident did not die down as quickly as some of Harry's other misdemeanours, however, and while he was forgiven a lot on the back of the tragic circumstances of his childhood, there was a feeling that this was of a different order. Harry didn't just have to make up for that episode; he had to prove that he was not the sort of person who would cause such offence. In the event, his time in the Army was to transform his public image and redeem him totally in the public eye.

Prince Charles accompanied Harry to Sandhurst, gave him an affectionate punch on the arm and was gone. His younger son was now one of 270 new recruits on the 44-week officer training course; he would be one of Alamein's three platoons of 30 men. Harry was to be referred to as 'Wales' by his fellow cadets; 'Mr Wales' or Officer Cadet Wales' by his senior officers. And by April 2006, less than a year after he entered Sandhurst, he had finished his officer training and was commissioned as a second lieutenant (cornet) in the Blues and Royals, a regiment of the Household Cavalry, with the service number 564673, where he became Captain Wales. On

13 April 2008, after he had been in the Army for two years, Harry was promoted to lieutenant.

The Army was to be the making of him, but of course life went on outside as well. The obsessive interest in him only intensified as he got older – as it did with William – and the memory of his mother was a constant that hovered over him, both in the great sense of loss he felt and the fact that people still associated him with the Princess. On the tenth anniversary of her death, Harry and William gave a joint interview on US television to Matt Lauer on NBC News in which they talked about their mother: Diana had 'always been there,' said Harry. 'It's weird because I think when she passed away there was never that time, there was never that sort of lull. There was never that sort of peace and quiet for any of us – the fact that her face was always splattered on the paper the whole time. You know, when people think about it, they think about her death. They think about how wrong it was. They think about whatever happened. Whatever happened in that tunnel – no one will ever know. And I'm sure people will always think about that the whole time.'

Harry referred to the fact that Diana would have wanted her two boys to lead a normal life. 'I think she'd be happy in the way that we're going about it, but slightly unhappy about the way the other people were going about it – as in saying, "Look, you're not normal, so stop trying to be normal", which is very much what we get a lot,' he said. 'It's like, "Stop trying to be normal. You've got certain responsibilities", which obviously we do, and we know we have certain responsibilities. But within our private life, and within certain other parts of our life, we want to be as normal as possible. And, yes, it's hard, because to a certain respect we never will be normal.'

The boys also talked about the problem of weeding out sycophants who were only interested in them because of who they were, and how it was also difficult for their real friends. 'Some of them are good at playing along,' said Harry. 'But at the same time, you've got to understand that it's just as hard for our friends as it is for us – there's a massive element of trust. You look surprised when I say that. But the reason I say that is because our friends have to put up with a lot – when it comes to us.'

And what would Harry like to do if he was not in the position he was in? 'No, honestly, I don't know how well this would get on but I'd probably live in Africa,' he said. 'I'd like to spend all my time out there. It would be a humanitarian aspect as well as a sort of safari aspect. I would have to get a job. So it would probably be a safari guide.'

That interview did actually cause a small backlash itself

in that Harry referred to the fact that the truth about the car crash that killed his mother would probably never be known. Conspiracy theories had been doing the rounds almost from the moment it had happened, with suspicions that shadowy forces had connived at Diana's death for any number of reasons, even including her relationship with Dodi Fayed. A Clarence House spokesman explained that he had been talking about whether anything could have prevented the crash, not what had made it happen. 'Of course, Prince Harry and Prince William will always be thinking a lot about what happened that night and whether the accident could have been avoided,' he said. 'But they have never doubted their mother's death was an accident. When the Stevens report came out last December, they said they hoped its conclusive findings would put an end to the speculation.'

Shortly before that interview was broadcast, the Ministry of Defence and Clarence House made a joint announcement that Harry would be sent to Iraq, as part of the 1st Mechanised Brigade of the 3rd Mechanised Division, which he had previously gone on the record as saying he wanted to do. 'There's no way I'm going to put myself through Sandhurst and then sit on my arse back home while my boys are out fighting for their country', he declared. But, as with everything pertaining to Harry, this, too, was fraught with controversy. There were concerns that he would be putting the lives of his fellow soldiers at risk because he would be a very specific target: 'The danger is that Prince Harry will be hazarding the lives of other soldiers and young officers and I think that's not right,' the former Conservative Defence Secretary told Radio 4's '*World at One*' and he certainly wasn't alone in this view. Nor was the timing ideal: two British soldiers had recently been killed doing the duties Harry would be expected to perform and a Challenger tank had just been attacked. The Ministry of Defence was adamant, however: 'It is still our intent that Prince Harry will deploy as a troop leader,' it said.

In the event, the then Head of the British Army, General Sir Richard Dannatt, stepped in to calm matters down: 'The decision has been taken by myself that he will deploy in due course,' Dannatt said. 'I would urge that the somewhat frenzied media activity surrounding this particular story should cease in the interests of the overall security of all our people deployed in Iraq.' Harry was scheduled for deployment in May or June 2007, to patrol the Maysan Governorate in southeastern Iraq.

But on 16 May there was a rethink and Harry was told he couldn't go after all. 'I have decided today that Prince Harry will not deploy as a troop commander with his squadron,' said Sir Richard. 'I have come to this final decision following a further and wide round of consultation, including a visit to Iraq by myself at the end of last week. There have been a number of specific threats, some reported and some not reported. These threats exposed him and those around him to a degree of risk I considered unacceptable. Let me also make quite clear that as a professional soldier, Prince Harry will be extremely disappointed. He has proved himself both at Sandhurst and in command of his troop during their training. I commend him for his determination and his undoubted talent – and I do not say that lightly. His soldiers will miss his leadership in Iraq, although I know his commanding officer will provide a highly capable substitute troop leader.'

Harry was indeed extremely disappointed, devastated even, by the decision: it had been his chance to prove himself and it seemed that his status was also holding him back in his chosen career. 'Prince Harry is very disappointed that he will not be able to go to Iraq with his troop on this deployment, as he had hoped,' a statement read. 'He fully understands and accepts Gen. Dannatt's difficult decision, and remains committed to his army career. Prince Harry's thoughts are with his troop and the rest of the Battle Group in Iraq.'

Behind the scenes, however, much stronger language

was used. 'It hit him badly, not being allowed to go to Iraq,' one officer who trained with Harry told the *Daily Telegraph*. 'Sandhurst was the beginning of the change in him. People see it as some sort of toff's finishing school. Not true. It's a melting pot. Only about 15 per cent come from public school and William and Harry did themselves a lot of good by mixing with the other 85 per cent and proving they could be good soldiers. Harry benefited most. He grew up at Sandhurst. When he was barred from active service, he felt it keenly.'

As a consolation prize, of sorts, in June 2007 Harry went to Canada to train alongside soldiers of the Canadian Forces and British Army, at CFB Suffield, near Medicine Hat, Alberta, and it was widely believed that this was in preparation for a tour of duty in Afghanistan, where Canadian and British forces were participating in the NATO-led Afghan War. In the meantime, he had other concerns. Harry and William had been involved in planning the Concert for Diana to mark the tenth anniversary of their mother's death, to be held on 1 July that year, on what would have been her forty-sixth birthday. William's girlfriend Kate Middleton and Harry's girlfriend Chelsy Davy (of whom more anon) were also said to be involved in the planning and the boys were to be the hosts.

The concert was a huge success. It was held in the newly built Wembley Stadium and was broadcast in 140 countries across the world, with an estimated audience of 500 million. The Princes, looking a little nervous, opened the show, and despite nerves Harry managed a joke: 'When William and I first had the idea, we forgot we would end up standing here desperately trying to think of something funny to say,' he said. 'We'll leave that to the funny people – and Ricky Gervais.' The performers included some of Diana's favourite performers as well as newer faces on the scene and it was a starry line-up indeed: Elton John, Duran Duran, James Morrison, Lily Allen, Tom Jones, Bryan Ferry, Donny Osmond and many more. The English National Ballet performed an excerpt from *Swan Lake* (Diana was a great ballet lover) and speakers included the two Princes, Kiefer Sutherland, Nelson Mandela (on video), Bill Clinton (on video) and Tony Blair. Harry addressed his colleagues in Iraq: 'I wish I was there with you,' he said. 'I'm sorry I can't be. But to all of those on operations at the moment, we'd both like to say – stay safe.' There were compensations – charities benefited, specifically charities supported by Princess Diana, as well the Diana Memorial Fund, Centrepoint and, of course, Sentebale.

But back in the day job, Harry wanted to fight as a

soldier as he had been trained to. And the following year the news emerged that after the disappointment of Iraq, he had indeed been serving in Helmand Province in Iraq. Initially he had gone to Forward Operating Base Dwyer, before moving on to Garmsir District, close to no man's land, on the other side of which were the Taliban. Had they known of Harry's presence so nearby, they would of course have had him down as a marked man. He was based in a madrasa (a college for Islamic instruction) alongside a Gurkha unit, working as a tactical air controller, which involved supporting ground forces with allied air cover, as well as going out on ground patrols. 'Just walking around, some of the locals or the ANP [Afghan National Police] they haven't got a clue who I am, they wouldn't know,' he said later.

He clearly loved every minute of it and joked about his 'bullet magnet' nickname: 'I haven't really had a shower for four days, I haven't washed my clothes for a week,' he said in footage once the news that he had been serving in Afghanistan emerged. 'It's very nice to be sort of a normal person for once. I think it's about as normal as I'm going to get. I am still a little bit conscious of the fact that if I show my face too much in and around the area… luckily there's no civilians around here because it's a no man's land. But I think that if, up north, when I do go up there, if I do go on patrols in amongst the locals, I'll still be very wary about the fact that I do need to keep my face slightly covered just on the off-chance that I do get recognised, which will put other guys in danger. The Gurkhas think it's hysterical how I am called the "bullet magnet", but they've yet to see why. [It's] a bit of excitement, a bit of phew, finally, [to] get the chance to actually do the soldiering that I wanted to do ever since I joined really.'

Harry was no figurehead. It emerged that he had taken part in a gun battle, helping the Gurkhas to repel the Taliban by firing a machine gun: 'It's just no man's land… They poke their heads up, that's it,' he crowed. He had become the first British Royal to serve in a war zone since his Uncle Andrew had flown helicopters in the Falklands War, and he had only been able to do so because the British and Canadian authorities imposed a news blackout that the international media initially respected.

However, in February 2008, the news leaked out, via the American Drudge Report website and then the German newspaper *Bild* and Australian magazine *New Idea*. General Dannatt was not pleased: 'I am very disappointed that foreign websites have decided to run this story without consulting us,' he said. 'This is in stark contrast to the highly responsible attitude that the whole of the UK print and broadcast media, along with a small number overseas, who have entered into an understanding with us over the coverage of Prince Harry on operations.' And of course now that his cover was blown, Harry had to leave Afghanistan, but he had had the service he wanted. It was also an indication to the public that there was a lot more to him than just being a hard-drinking party boy. He had served his country and made it proud. The newspapers had a different name for him: 'Hero Harry', they said. Harry was also rewarded for his bravery: he was presented with an Operational Service Medal for Afghanistan by his aunt, Princess Anne, at the Combermere Barracks in May 2008.

Harry's performance in Afghanistan had been exemplary and in October 2008 Clarence House announced that he was to be 'graded' in order to decide whether he could start the full Army Air Corps (AAC) programme and, following in the footsteps of his brother, father and uncle, learn to pilot military helicopters. This was a serious move: about half the candidates failed to make the grade and the initial four-week course entailed thirteen hours of flying. If the candidate shows proper progress, then they embark on a full training course lasting sixteen months. Harry passed his test at the

AAC base in Middle Wallop and went on to train alongside William at the Defence Helicopter Flying School at RAF Shawbury.

The relationship between the Royals and the armed forces is a close one: having already been presented with a medal by his aunt, on 7 May 2010, at a ceremony at the Army Air Corps Base, Middle Wallop, Harry was presented with his flying brevet (wings) by his father, with Chelsy Davy and his two maternal aunts attending the ceremony. He was to learn to fly Apache attack helicopters: 'It is a huge honour to have the chance to train on the Apache, which is an awesome helicopter,' he said. 'There is still a huge mountain for me to climb if I am to pass the Apache training course. To be honest, I think it will be one of the biggest challenges in my life so far. I am very determined, though, as I do not want to let down people who have shown faith in my ability to fly this aircraft on operations. It is a seriously daunting prospect but I can't wait.'

Harry made the grade, being told by the military that he had a 'natural flair' for flying. He was awarded his Apache Flying Badge on 14 April 2011 and was promoted to captain, which entailed a pay rise from £37,916 to £45,000, amid further speculation that he would return to Afghanistan; to that end he was put on an eight-month training course teaching him how to use the Apache's weapons in battle. These included rockets, missiles and an automatic canon. Harry badly wanted to go: his 'heart was in the army,' he said. No shirker he: 'I'd just be taking up a spare place for somebody else if they didn't have me going out on the job.'

He was sent to a US base in California to complete his training, splitting his time between the Naval Air Facility El Centro and the Gila Bend Air Force Auxiliary Field in Arizona: once Harry was 'combat ready' he was almost certain to return to Afghanistan. More reports surfaced about his prowess: he came top of his class and was now described as an 'exceptional' pilot. 'There are many skills needed to be a top-drawer Apache pilot but apparently it's Harry's flying that is particularly impressive,' an army source told the *Daily Telegraph*. 'His handling, hand–eye co-ordination, reaction speeds – he's a natural.'

Harry completed his training at Wattisham Flying Station in Suffolk, and in September 2012 flew to Camp Bastion in southern Afghanistan as part of the 100-strong 662 Squadron, 3 Regiment, Army Air Corps, to begin a four-month combat tour to take part in missions against the Taliban. The Taliban were not slow to issue threats: Taliban spokesman Zabiullah Mujahid told Reuters: 'We are using all our strength to get rid of him, either by killing or kidnapping… We have informed our commanders in Helmand to do whatever they can to eliminate him.'

On 21 January 2013, it was announced that Harry was returning from a twenty-week deployment in Afghanistan and on 8 July 2013, the Ministry of Defence announced that he had successfully qualified as an Apache aircraft commander. He had passed with 'flying colours' according to his regiment's commanding officer, Lieutenant Colonel Tom de la Rue, and was now at the very top of his profession. And had Captain Wales been a member of any other family, it is entirely possible that that is where he would have stayed, because as Harry himself understood, the Armed Forces had provided him not only with the opportunity to prove himself, but also to live the nearest thing possible to a normal life – if flying Apache helicopters against the Taliban can in any way be considered normal. But Harry was a Royal and the normal rules did not apply. His time in the Army was coming to an end; thought was now being given to what he would do with the rest of his life.

CHAPTER 11

FIRST LOVE

Like Meghan, Harry also had a backstory when it came to romance. Ever since he was a young man, he had had an eye for the ladies. That early relationship with Emma Lippiatt had petered out years previously, but before meeting Meghan, Harry was to have two serious girlfriends. He was clearly happiest with a woman at his side, and the first of those two women, with whom he was to have an on-off relationship for seven years, was Chelsy Davy.

Harry met Chelsy when he was on his gap year, prior to his army days, during a visit to Cape Town in early 2004. She was born on 13 October 1985 in Bulawayo, Zimbabwe, to Charles Davy, a South African with a safari business, and Beverley Donald Davy, who had been a model for Coca-Cola, and Miss Rhodesia (as Zimbabwe was formerly called) in 1973. Here, as so often, Harry managed to court controversy, albeit entirely not of his own making – when the relationship came to light, eyebrows were raised when it emerged that Charles Davy was close to the controversial Zimbabwean President Robert Mugabe. Enormously rich, with huge land holdings, he was also close to the controversial Webster Shamu, who was the minister responsible for policy implementation. They ran a business together and when questioned about this, Charles said, 'I am in partnership with a person who I personally like and get along with.' He further denounced stories about him as 'a spate of rubbish', adding that 'I am in business, not politics.' However, he later sold his share in the business.

Chelsy grew up in a form of paradise. The family homestead was in the Lemco Safari Area in Matabeleland, which covered about 1,300 square miles and included a thatch-covered building with a swimming pool and tennis court. Herds of game roamed through the grounds; Charles – regrettably, considering Harry and William's future animal conservation campaign work – ran hunting safaris on the land. It was here that Harry developed his love of the vast open spaces of Africa, although his beloved also had strong links to the UK.

Chelsea spent a brief period at Cheltenham College (not Cheltenham Ladies' College) and went on to Stowe, before studying Politics, Philosophy and Economics at the University of Cape Town (funnily enough, all Harry's girlfriends, including Meghan, reached a higher level of education than him). She was there between 2003 and 2006 and the following year went to Leeds University to study law.

Harry rarely gave interviews about his girlfriend, although behind the scenes it was reportedly a tempestuous relationship. But he did sometimes relent. On his twenty-first birthday, he described Chelsy as 'very special… I would love to tell everyone how amazing she is. But, you know, that is my private life and once I start talking about that, then I've left my own self open, and if anyone asks me in the future, then they'll say, "Oh well, hang on, you told them but why aren't you telling us?"'

From the start there were spats, including a major one when Harry missed Chelsy's twenty-second birthday in order to attend the Rugby World Cup Final in Paris. But she and Harry were actually extremely well suited. Although Chelsy was credited with 'taming' him – and it is true that Harry's reputation began to improve quite significantly once they were together – she clearly liked to party as much as he did. She enjoyed a drink and a cigarette and, coming from the type of background she did, where hard living was the norm, seemed the ideal consort for Harry the man about town. But the relationship was marked with drama, with splits and reconciliations, and although Harry's brother William had also briefly split with Kate Middleton, their relationship was a deeper one and built to endure. One problem was that while Kate seemed to be able to cope with all the attention that being involved with a prince entailed, Chelsy did not. They were also both very young.

Harry celebrated the end of his training at Sandhurst with a visit to a lap dancing club, which did not go down well, and nor did pictures of him kissing barmaids when he was on a training course in Canada. That last led to a brief break before a kiss and make up. Not that Chelsy was averse to a flirtation of her own, as pictures of her with Jabu Kirkland, the scion of a rich Cape Town family, taken when Harry was in Afghanistan, made clear. After the Canada episode, however, she was so angry that Harry whisked her off to Botswana, where the pair agreed she would come to the UK to study at Leeds.

But she provided a huge amount of emotional support to Harry, not least during his travails when he thought he would not be allowed to go out and fight. 'There is no doubt about it, there is a very, very strong bond between them,' a former Royal aide told the *Daily Telegraph*. 'And to understand it you have to look at the background. When his mother died Harry felt dreadfully emotionally exposed. In the years that followed, he felt very keenly that "second son" syndrome. He has always been that little bit forgotten. The Prince of Wales is an extremely loving father but he failed to notice as swiftly as Princess Diana would have that Harry needed an extra dose of attention.'

Another Royal source agreed. 'She helped him deal with the Iraq thing,' he said. 'But she was able to explain to him that he must not see the Iraq thing as a setback. That a dignified and grown-up response was what was required from him. That he could bemoan not being sent, but show his responsible nature by saying he understood that his presence would put his comrades at increased risk. She was, literally, the only one from whom he could accept that advice.'

The bond between them was indeed strong, but sadly not enough to survive the problems they were going to have to face. For a start, Chelsy's family, while very attached to Harry himself, were not deliriously happy about some aspects of the relationship: it had brought unwelcome attention to her father's business concerns and the family also commented on the fact that while

Harry always had a protection officer around him, Chelsy did not.

The move to Leeds, where she was accompanied by her mother Beverley, who helped her to settle in, might have been expected to make the couple happier, as they were now at least on the same continent, but it did not. Chelsy was said to be unhappy in the northern city: for all its undoubted charms, to a person used to life in the African outback, this must have come as something of a shock. The climate was different from what she was used to and there were not the same opportunities for an outdoor life: 'It has been difficult for her moving to Leeds, leaving all her friends, especially her brother Shaun, and starting all over again,' a friend told the *Daily Mail*. 'It was all quite emotional. I don't think she has many friends there and is keeping a lot to herself.' In Cape Town she lived in an apartment overlooking the ocean; in Leeds she was close to crime-ridden areas with no view, although it was her own decision – while she could easily have afforded to live somewhere much grander, she wanted to be close to her fellow students. 'This area is where all the students tend to congregate and Chelsy wanted to make sure she was able to fit in,' one of her fellow students told a newspaper. 'She didn't want to be in a posh part of town, where she would be cutting herself off from other students.'

But it was not a happy way to live. Nor was she seeing a great deal of Harry, who had just started his full AAC training, with the strong implication that relationships came second. Given that Chelsy had moved to Leeds to be closer to him, this was something of a slap in the face. This unhappiness began to become more public. When she returned home for Christmas, she posted on Facebook, 'Chelsy is SO ridiculously happy to be back!' In January this changed to, 'Chelsy doesn't wanna go!'

Matters finally came to a head. After Chelsy was pictured in tears at a London nightclub, it emerged that the couple had decided to go their separate ways in January 2009. There was no question that there was still a very strong attachment, but circumstances were making it impossible and she did it in the most modern of ways, by changing her relationship status on Facebook to 'single'. There was no comment from the Palace.

'She kept saying she needed to take some time out to re-establish herself,' a friend told the *Daily Mail*. 'She still loves him, but she feels she needs to carve an identity as her own person rather than as Prince Harry's girlfriend. Over recent weeks she's been coming down to London and partying with Harry's friends. They were together at Amika nightclub in Kensington just two weeks ago when Chelsy appeared incredibly down and subdued. She was not her normal partying self. She had confided it was because she was missing Zimbabwe and her family in South Africa, but in fact she was having doubts about her relationship with Prince Harry back then. While they care for each other deeply she needs to be able to be her own person. She is pragmatic about the split. They're using it as an opportunity to take a break rather than splitting for good.'

It was the first real example of a problem that Harry was going to encounter again: while in theory no one is more eligible than a prince, in practice, the attention it brings can be very difficult to deal with. While on the one hand Chelsy cultivated a fun-loving image, on the other she clearly preferred the attention she garnered to be confined to her personal life and not splashed across the front pages of the newspapers. She was also a contributory factor in the changing public image of her on-and-off boyfriend – from little boy lost to bad boy to fearless soldier capable of an emotionally mature relationship – but the big problem was that she wanted to be private. So, if it comes to that, did William's girlfriend Kate Middleton, but she appeared to be able to deal with the ongoing fascination with her relationship to the heir to the throne in a way Chelsy did not.

Both girls had to deal with another factor, as well:

the innate snobbishness of some parts of the British public, especially that sector of it that was engaged in all things royal. Kate Middleton's humble background was constantly raked over, especially the fact that her mother had once been an air stewardess, with the viciously nasty murmur of 'Doors to manual' accompanying her wherever she went. (Although Kate did turn out to have the last laugh.)

With Chelsy it was just as bad, although in a slightly different way. She did not come from a humble background, quite the opposite, but there were the usual rumblings about 'nouveau riche'. And while Kate had a prim air about her, Chelsy did not. Quite the opposite: she came across as the ultimate party girl and that jarred with many people's idea of a typical princess. The journalist and author Tom Sykes summed it up perfectly when he said that Chelsy's blonde and tanned appearance made her look 'like she's at one end or the other of a four-day bender. Because she looks like she's always on her way to a sorority Hallowe'en party, people kind of don't take her seriously,' he told ABCNews.com. Even her name was a problem, not least because the fashionable London district it referred to was actually spelt Chelsea: 'Chelsy was this very aspirational name that was originally meant to be all class but then got totally appropriated by the cockneys, the lower-class, the chav culture,' Sykes added. 'It is almost completely impossible for the British public to imagine a princess called Chelsy. It's one of those things that shouldn't matter that really, really does matter so much.'

It would have been difficult enough for anyone to deal with, but for someone who lived on the other half of the world from her original friends and family, and who was having to cope with homesickness, a cold and grey climate and a boyfriend who was away a lot of the time on either military or Royal duties, it was just too much. For a while, it really did seem as if this was the end of the line. 'Chelsy's heart is with her family and Africa,' a friend told the *Daily Mail*. 'She comes from a relaxed family with different values and a completely different lifestyle from the royals. This is what Harry loves about her. The irony is that ultimately this is why they can never be together for ever. She has often told her friends she will never marry him not only because she doesn't, ultimately, want to live in England but also because she doesn't want the attention that comes with dating a royal. She wants a normal life.'

And ironically, it was Chelsy who was concerned about Harry's status, not vice versa. 'It's not just that Chelsy's not interested in becoming a princess,' the same friend told the *Daily Mail*. 'She actively doesn't want it. For her, Harry being royal gets in the way of them being together and has no benefits at all. Chelsy and Harry have always been happier together away from all that fuss in her homeland, not his.'

Chelsy was then seen out on the town with the thirty-three-year-old property developer Dan Philipson and given that they were visiting nightclubs where they were almost bound to be noticed, it is clear she was making a point. Harry was said to be devastated, but the relationship only lasted a couple of months.

Nor did Harry pine too much himself. He reportedly had a brief relationship with the television presenter Caroline Flack, who clearly had a bit of a thing for both younger men and blokes called Harry – she was also linked to One Direction's Harry Styles. That didn't last long either. In her autobiography she said that they'd met through a friend, but it wasn't really a relationship – 'To meet a prince is so unlikely it would be weird not to acknowledge it,' she wrote. 'However, once the story got out, that was it. We had to stop seeing each other. I was no longer Caroline Flack, TV presenter, I was Caroline Flack, Prince Harry's bit of rough.'

The Prince and the party girl were not quite done, however, and started an on-again, off-again bout in their romance, which neither seemed able to break out of. Chelsy graduated from Leeds in 2009 and returned to Africa, and it was by no means certain that she would return to the UK. She had previously been an intern with Farrer & Company, the Queen's solicitors, and in the natural course of things it would have been normal for her to have returned there to take her articles in order to qualify as a solicitor, but a period of indecision followed. Chelsy took another gap year, travelling around South Africa, Zimbabwe, Zambia, Mauritius and Australia while she decided what she actually wanted to do.

However, behind the scenes she and Harry reconciled and it then appeared that they had split again. Chelsy tended to be around for the big occasions, but once matters seemed to be turning serious again, she was gone in a puff of smoke.

On 29 April 2011 Harry's elder brother William got married to Kate Middleton at Westminster Abbey in a ceremony watched by hundreds of millions of viewers around the world. Harry professed himself to be delighted when the couple got engaged: 'It means I get a sister, which I have always wanted,' he said. Royal grooms usually have 'supporters' rather than a best man, but William broke with tradition and had the latter, in this case Harry, resplendent in the uniform of a captain of the Blues and Royals, sporting aiguillettes, a cross belt and gold waist belt; he wore the wings of the Army Air Corps and Golden Jubilee and Afghanistan campaign medals. Although military dress uniforms do not usually have pockets, the Palace asked for a special modification to Harry's uniform to allow him to carry the bride's wedding ring. There was a sprinkling of bridesmaids and page boys as well as a maid of honour, namely Kate's sister Pippa, who almost stole the show, appearing in a figure-hugging Alexander McQueen outfit that showed off her curves.

Given Harry's reputation as a ladies' man and the fact that the two clearly got on well together, laughing and joking once the solemnity of the wedding was over and the celebrations had begun, many onlookers decided that Harry's ideal girlfriend might actually be none other than Pippa herself. There was a lunch at Buckingham Palace hosted by the Queen followed by an appearance on the Palace's balcony involving all the main players, including Harry and Pippa, during which the happy couple delighted onlookers with the traditional kiss. In the evening Prince Charles hosted a dinner followed by a dance; it was a display of the personal mixed up with pageantry in a style that the British Royal family manages *par excellence*.

But far from Harry finding his perfect match in Pippa, he was actually with Chelsy throughout. She was in the Abbey and there at every part of the celebrations, and according to onlookers, she and Harry were all over each other before the party broke up at around 3am and they retired to the nearby Goring hotel, where the Middleton family was staying. Could it have been that it took another wedding to finally make them realise how important they were to one another?

No. Important to one another they might have been, but Chelsy had seen the crowds up close, the hysteria that Kate and William provoked and the absolute certainty that that is the attention that they too would attract. The balcony of Buckingham Palace is a long way from the savannas of southern Africa and it seemed to bring it home to Chelsy once and for all that this was not the life for her. Harry's appeals were to be in vain.

'Chelsy and Harry are back together and it was very significant that she was his plus one for the day,' a friend told the *Daily Mail*. 'Harry adores Chelsy and really wants things to work. He has brought up marriage in the past but Chelsy's the one to quickly play it all down. She has watched what Kate has gone through and how much she has had to sacrifice, and says it's not for her. Chelsy thought the wedding was wonderful and she had a ball, but there's no way marriage is on the cards for her. She wants her freedom and to start a career. That's her focus at the moment, she and Harry are going to see how things go.'

Chelsy then took up a place at the solicitors firm Allen & Overy (which had helped Edward VIII during the Abdication crisis) to complete her articles, the two-year training every lawyer must do before they become a fully qualified solicitor. This was a very prestigious firm to work for and again brought home the fact that Chelsea was far more than just a pretty face; she was also back in a considerably more anonymous world, which clearly suited her. For a girl with a flamboyant personal style, she was surprisingly keen to remain in the background.

And although law might have seemed a surprising profession for someone who was an outdoors-loving party girl, Chelsy was pursuing a childhood dream. 'I wanted to be a lawyer from a young age,' she told *Country & Town House* magazine several years later. 'I think it was when I was about nine years old and saw *A Few Good Men* that my fate was sealed. I followed those ambitions and qualified as a solicitor at Allen & Overy. I enjoyed the challenge and really appreciated the opportunity to work with some brilliant legal minds. It also made me fully aware of the capacity we have when we push ourselves to the limit (and how little sleep we can survive on!).'

Harry, meanwhile, accepted that the relationship was over, this time for good. A couple of months after the wedding, he was spotted at a Hard Rock Calling concert in Hyde Park, where he was quizzed over that obvious chemistry with Pippa. 'Pippa? Ha! No, I am not seeing anyone at the moment. I'm 100 per cent single,' he revealed at the Live Nation VIP lounge. 'I'm working a lot at the moment, so dating and watching TV are the last things I have time for.'

Harry and Chelsy remained on good terms: neither has ever said a bad word about the other. A few years later Harry was seen with Chelsy's family in South Africa and it was clear to his friends that he carried a torch for her for years: it was a case of right girl, wrong circumstance. Despite repeated rumours of a reconciliation, it never came to be. 'I think [Harry and I] will always be good friends,' Chelsy subsequently told *The Sunday Times*, but added that life in the public eye 'is not something you get used to'.

Chelsy did not, however, continue with the law: in 2014, after three years with Allen & Overy, she decided to launch her own ethical jewellery range. Named AYA, it was based in London and used gems mined in Zambia.

She had decided she wanted to run her own business and studied at the Gemological Institute of America before branching out on her own.

'I have spent a lot of time travelling through Africa, but it was when I saw a Zambian emerald for the first time that my curiosity for African gemstones was really ignited, so I decided to study gemology at the Gemological Institute of America,' Chelsy told *Country & Town House*. 'The more I learnt, the more fascinated I became. And so AYA was born. I want to facilitate change, that's why I work with Gemfields to source the finest gemstones ethically. Education is key, so AYA is committed to improving the quality and accessibility of schooling in local communities across Africa.'

Chelsy based herself, fittingly, in Chelsea, from where she runs the business and travels the world. Whether she will ever return to the wide open plains of Africa to live there permanently is not yet clear. But she remains Harry's first real love – and made her mark on the heart of a prince.

CHAPTER 12

A SOLDIER AND A PRINCE

Harry was to have two long-term relationships before he met Meghan Markle. But in the two-year gap between those relationships, he seemed to find it increasingly difficult to find the right person. With his brother clearly happily settled down, he became a little disconsolate. At the end of a very successful tour of Latin America in March 2012 to launch the Queen's Diamond Jubilee celebrations, he said, somewhat wistfully, 'I'm not so much searching for someone to fulfil the role, but obviously, you know, finding someone that would be willing to take it on.' Did being a Royal live up to the popular image? 'No, not at all, ha ha – as any girl would ever tell you. It's sort of, "Oh my god, he's a prince."

But no. The job that it entails – I mean look at me, I'm twenty-seven years old.'

Desolate words. But as so often happens, just when someone has given up on finding love, along it comes, and so Harry's second series relationship began shortly afterwards when his cousin, Princess Eugenie, introduced him to Cressida Bonas in May 2012. A very pretty blonde, Cressida Curzon Bonas was born on 18 February 1989 and so was a few years younger than her new beau; she also had a boho/aristo background that thrilled the media when the relationship became public.

She is the youngest daughter of Lady Mary-Gaye Curzon and her former husband, the entrepreneur Jeffrey Bonas; her mother had been an 'It girl' in the 1960s, and has a string of marriages to her name. Cressida's grandfather was Edward Curzon, the sixth Earl Howe. Her father had also been married more than once, which meant she has seven half-siblings, including the actress Isabella Anstruther Gough Calthorpe, who is now married to Sam Branson, another friend of the young Royals. It was rumoured that Lady Curzon was delighted when the news emerged of her daughter's new beau. For a time it seemed that marriage was on the cards and bohemian as the family was, marriage to a senior member of the Royal family was not an unwelcome prospect. But it was not to be.

Intriguingly, like Meghan, Cressida is an actress. Born in Winchester and educated at Prior Park College in Bath before going on to Stowe, she studied dance at Leeds University and post-graduate dance at the Trinity Laban Conservatoire in Greenwich, South London and it was while still at school that she developed the acting bug. She played the cockney housekeeper Mrs Swabb in *Habeas Corpus* by Alan Bennett: 'Cressida Bonas moved beautifully around the stage,' wrote her drama teacher. '[She] controlled the action so well, acting as a narrator and onstage scene shifter. The baggy Nora Batty style tights will be an abiding memory for me!' She also played the lead role in August Strindberg's *Miss Julie* and Laura in *The Glass Menagerie* by Tennessee Williams. By the time she met Harry, Cressida had already started to establish herself and had made her screen debut in 2009 in the drama series *Trinity*. Somewhat inevitably, she too had been dubbed an 'It girl', albeit one who was set on a career.

However, there were some differences between the couple. Harry was in his late twenties; Cressida was younger, just starting out and quite overwhelmed by all the attention. Early on in their relationship, matters were not helped by a very embarrassing incident involving her new boyfriend: on a trip to Las Vegas Harry and his entourage started chatting to a group of women in their hotel bar.

The party adjourned to Harry's suite, where a game of strip pool was suggested, and in no time at all the young Prince and assorted hangers-on were naked. It seems that Harry's security detail had not confiscated the gathering's mobile phones: pictures were taken and soon afterwards appeared on the celebrity website TMZ. From there they went straight to the world's press, although papers in the UK were a little more circumspect about using them. The Royal family's spokesman was forced to confirm that yes, it was Harry, and promptly contacted the Press Complaints Committee to try to prevent the pictures from being published in the UK. Harry himself went to ground and it was only in an interview a couple of months later that the Prince revealed his mortification. 'At the end of the day I probably let myself down, I let my family down, I let other people down...' he said. 'But it was probably a classic example of me probably being too much army, and not enough prince. It's a simple case of that.' It didn't do his standing with the public much harm. Opinion polls conducted in November 2012 showed Harry to be the third most popular member of the Royal family, after the Queen and William.

One of the other people Harry let down was, of course, Cressida, but in that same interview he gave a strong impression that at this point at least the Army was very much his priority. There were 'three mes' he said, adding, 'One in the army, one socially in my own private time, and then one with the family and stuff like that. So there is a switch and I flick it when necessary. And I'd like to think that it's measured and balanced as the way it is [...] I think, to be honest with you, it's the role for anybody in the army, especially the role for myself and William – you've got to be able to flip the switch all the time.'

And he was not settling down just yet. 'Army comes first,' he insisted. 'It's my work at the end of the day.' Asked if he felt more comfortable as Captain Wales than Prince Harry, he replied, 'Definitely. I've always been like that. My father's always trying to remind me about who I am and stuff like that. But it's very easy to forget about who I am when I am in the army. Everyone's wearing the same uniform and doing the same kind of thing.'

Despite this, for a time there was speculation that he and Cressida might settle down. Harry introduced her to other members of the Royal family and they were seen canoodling at a party for his Uncle Andrew's birthday. The bookies, unusually, got this one wrong and slashed the odds on them getting engaged. The pair attended a Royal event together, We Day, which benefited the Free The Children charity, and appeared natural and affectionate in public. They were seen at a James Blunt concert, in the audience at the musical *The Book Of Mormon*; there was also a visit to the Queen's Scottish residence at Sandringham, something usually only accorded to serious significant others. Rather more ominously there was talk that Cressida was thinking of giving up her career, and whether or not that was actually ever true, the mere speculation might have been enough to give her cold feet.

Then there was Harry's career to worry about, too. There was a dangerous precedent within the Royal family as to what could happen to a prince who leaves the Armed Forces and doesn't find another fulfilling role. That precedent was created by Prince Andrew, who himself had been a heart-throb prince and military hero, having served in the Falklands War. But his reputation had been badly tarnished in later life, not just through the somewhat controversial image of his ex-wife, Sarah Ferguson, but because he had become known as 'Airmiles Andy', with a reputation for freeloading. And while he did have some nebulous role as a champion of British industry, he was perceived to spend more time on the golf course than anywhere else, which did not go down well with the wider public.

It was essential that Harry should avoid that fate, and as time went on, matters looked more promising. He started travelling extensively through the Commonwealth, representing the Royal family and becoming increasingly popular as he did so, not least because as he matured, his reserves of natural charm were becoming ever more obvious to the public. His charitable work and continuing role in the Army soon began to overshadow the Las Vegas incident and in 2014 he embarked on the hugely successful challenge of the Invictus Games. It was a further step forward in the changing public perception of Harry as a sometimes thoughtless young man to *homme sérieux*.

Harry first got the idea for the Invictus Games, an international Paralympic-style sporting competition for wounded, injured or sick Armed-Forces personnel, after he saw a British team competing at the US Warrior Games in Colorado in 2013; he decided to bring the concept to the UK. Such was the strength of his conviction that he stepped down as an Army Air Corps helicopter pilot to work on the launch, which took place on 6 March 2014 at London's Copper Box Arena, very much supported by the great and good. Backed also by the then London Mayor, Boris Johnson, the Ministry of Defence and the

London Organising Committee of the Olympic and Paralympic Games, sponsored by Jaguar Land Rover, and funded by among others, the Royal Foundation, a charity established by Harry, William and Kate and the Treasury, it was clear from the outset that this was to be a major new venture.

It would 'have a long-lasting impact' on those who fought for their country, said Harry. 'I have witnessed first-hand how the power of sport can positively impact the lives of wounded, injured and sick servicemen and women in their journey of recovery. The Invictus Games will focus on what they can achieve post-injury and celebrate their fighting spirit through an inclusive sporting competition that recognises the sacrifice they have made. I am extremely proud to be bringing an event like this to the UK for the first time and believe it can have a long-lasting impact on the well-being of those who have served their nations so bravely.'

The sports involved included athletics, archery, indoor rowing, powerlifting, road cycling, sitting volleyball, swimming, wheelchair basketball and wheelchair rugby. (The first games took place in London, after which they moved to Orlando in 2016 and Toronto the following year, and it was while in Toronto to discuss preparations in 2016 that Harry met Meghan Markle.)

Back in 2014, and just over a month after the launch it was reported that Harry and Cressida Bonas had split up; Cressida had never been comfortable in the full glare of the spotlight and there were further reports that she did not want to give up on her career, which she almost certainly would have had to do had she and Harry got married.

There was initially some speculation that they would get back together. After all, William and Kate had split up briefly before getting back together and getting engaged. But as the level of discomfort Cressida had been feeling became ever more clear, this seemed less likely. Friends spoke about how much she hated having complete strangers whip their phones out and take pictures of her.

However, Harry had matured a lot over the course of their two-year relationship and the feeling was that he now very much wanted to settle down and focus on his life's ambitions. His life was increasingly taken up with charity work, which was clearly where his future lay.

In March 2015 it was announced that he would be leaving the Armed Forces in June but before he did so he would spend four weeks in April and May seconded to the Australian Defence Force (ADF), at the Army barracks in Darwin, Perth and Sydney. After leaving the Army, he would return to work with the Ministry of Defence, supporting case officers in the Ministry of Defence's Recovery Capability Programme, working with both those who administer and receive physical and mental care within the London District area in a voluntary capacity, which of course very much fitted in with the work he had done with Invictus.

On 6 April 2015, Prince Harry reported for duty to Australia's Chief of the Defence Force, Air Chief Marshal Mark Binskin at the Royal Military College, Duntroon in Canberra, Australia, and then later flew to Darwin to start his month-long secondment to the ADF's 1st Brigade. During his time in Perth, he trained with Special Air Service Regiment (SASR), participating in the SASR selection course, and joined SASR members in Perth for live fire shooting exercises. In Sydney, he undertook urban operations training with the 2nd Commando Regiment. He spent time flying over Sydney as co-pilot of an Army Black Hawk and participated in counter-terrorism training in Sydney Harbour with Royal Australian Navy clearance divers. By then it was nearly over: Harry's attachment with the ADF ended on 8 May 2015 and on 19 June 2015 his career with the Army ended for good.

Back on civvy street, Harry's popularity continued to soar. Sometimes with William and Kate, sometimes on his own, he had started to split his time between representing the Royal family at official events, as he had also done when he was in the Army, and further charitable work – namely his charity, Sentebale.

'It started really really small… a very small group of us saying we're not going to use the funds for other people, it's going to be all for the kids and pretending we knew what we were doing,' Harry told MailOnline. 'Ten years down the line we have made a couple of mistakes and in turn learned from our mistakes and now we know that actually, by speaking to the core problem, which in this case is the children themselves, you get a really good taste of whether you're achieving it or not. The great thing about Lesotho is that because it's so small, you know that if you're doing it wrong, it's highly visible. And if you're doing it right, you start to see the change.'

Speaking at a polo match to raise funds for the charity, he continued, 'It's a very small country that no one knows about, surrounded by South Africa, a landlocked country, and I think that combined with us thinking that we knew what we were doing right, it evolved and it changed for the better. We realised our mistakes and we were willing to change it by speaking to the kids on the ground. What I'd like to think is that Sentebale has brought everyone together to work for one great cause. It's been an emotional rollercoaster but we've come out on top and all I've ever wanted to do was raise enough money to make a difference for Lesotho.' He hadn't, of course, met Meghan Markle at that point, but this was exactly the sort of thing she was also interested in, a clear sign from early on that the two were to have a great deal in common.

Everywhere Harry went he was mobbed, whether it was to his beloved Africa, often in support of Sentebale, to Kathmandu, to the Caribbean, Florida, centenary commemorations for the Battle of the Somme. He took part in activities that would have been inconceivable for a member of the Royal family until very recently. Of course, as previously mentioned, Princess Diana had been a pioneer in breaking the taboos around AIDS: she had been pictured in 1987 shaking hands with an HIV-positive dying patient, at a time when there was still a great deal of fear and ignorance about the disease and the misapprehension that mere skin-on-skin contact could constitute a risk. And more and more it seemed to be Harry, not his brother, who had been blessed with his mother's natural charm and ability to put people at their ease, although in fairness, William, the future monarch, was more constrained by his position. The formality that surrounded William was deemed necessary in many quarters, whereas Harry, increasingly pushed further down the line to the throne as William's family started to grow, was able to present a far more relaxed and lighthearted face to the world.

And who could not continue to sympathise with either of them? As William and Harry grew older they began to break with other more formal Royal family modes of behaviour, not least in talking about their mother, which now, in their thirties, they were able to do. 'I don't have that many memories of my childhood with my mum,' Harry told *People* magazine. 'I don't say "Right, I'm going to get involved in that because that's what my mum would want me to do", though inevitably once I'm doing it, I think "Do you know what? She'd probably love this."'

But that was perhaps in part because he'd buried so much. 'I never really dealt with what had happened,' he explained in an ITV documentary about his charity work in Lesotho in December 2016. 'It was a lot of buried emotion. For a huge part of my life I didn't really want to think about it. I now view life very differently from what it used to be. I used to bury my head in the sand, and let everything around tear me to pieces. I was fighting the system, going: "I don't want to be this person." My mother died when I was very, very young and I don't want to be in this position. Now I'm so energised, fired up, to be lucky enough to be in a position to make a difference.' He also later discussed the issues he faced after his mother's death with writer Bryony Gordon, author of *Mad Girl*, as part of a mental health awareness campaign attached to his patronage of the 'Heads Together' charity, in 2017.

By the time Harry met Meghan Markle in 2016, the transformation from party prince to philanthropist was complete. Early concerns that a lack of self-discipline combined with a wayward streak would make him one of the more unfocused members of the Royal family had given way to a perception of him as a principled young man with a sense of duty, supporting not only the Invictus Games, but also the HALO Trust, the London Marathon Charitable Trust and Walking With The Wounded, among many others. And alongside his brother and sister-in-law, Harry put a special emphasis on mental-health concerns, again another area that had concerned his mother. The fact that he was a prince concerned with duty and not just pleasure only enhanced his already high standing in the public eye – and made it more likely than ever that he would be indulged if he chose a bride from a rather different background from his own.

The huge change in the public perception of Harry was illustrated in the most unlikely possible fashion recently. In March 2017, Harry, along with most of the senior members of the Royal family, including the Queen (aged ninety), Prince Philip (aged ninety-five), Prince Charles and the Duchess of Cornwall, attended the annual Commonwealth Day service at Westminster Abbey. It was known to be an extremely important occasion for the Queen, who is head of the Commonwealth, an organisation of fifty-two countries, most of which were once part of the British Empire. With Britain's departure from the European Union on the cards, the Commonwealth was assuming an even greater importance in the life of the nation than ever before. The Queen was resplendent in canary yellow. Harry, showing the ability that came straight from his mother to connect with almost anyone, delighted a well-wisher, sixteen-year-old Rebecca Thornton, who has profound hearing difficulties and uses sign language, by high-fiving her as he left.

However, two people were mysteriously absent: Prince William, the second in line to the throne, and his wife, the Duchess of Cambridge. Where could they be? onlookers asked. What could conceivably have kept them away from such an important event? The Countess of Wessex, Prince Edward's wife, wasn't there either, but she was known to be representing the Queen in Malawi, which was as good an excuse as any for not showing up.

The explanation for the Cambridges' absence, which

emerged almost immediately, could not have been more embarrassing. William, who had already faced accusations of being work-shy, had chosen to take a skiing weekend with the boys – Guy Pelly, James Meade and Tom van Straubenzee – in Verbier, Switzerland. Worse still, he was pictured 'dad dancing' at the Farinet nightclub in the company of some very pretty models hours after high-fiving the Australian model Sophie Taylor in the course of a relaxed lunch in the restaurant La Vache. There was no suggestion that anything had gone on, but the pictures exposed the normally reserved William to ridicule. They would have been commented upon whenever they had been taken, but to miss the Commonwealth Day service for this drew real concerns that the Prince was neglecting his Royal duties. He was a thirty-four-year-old monarch -in-waiting and, as such should have known better. And to cap it all, his antics threatened to overshadow a forthcoming trip he and Kate were making to Paris, just a few months short of the twentieth anniversary of his mother's death in that very city.

But who was there to uphold the reputation of the Royal family, to show its ability to represent the people, to make it clear that duty to one's country came first? Harry. And that wasn't all he was doing that week. In the next few days after the service, he was helping pupils plant trees in Epping Forest, presenting models to Gurkhas and attending a Veterans' Mental Health Conference, where he met former serviceman Karl Hinett, who survived being torched by a mob in Iraq at the age of nineteen. Mental health issues are 'not a life sentence,' said Harry. 'It is incredibly difficult to talk about mental health in the armed forces,' he went on. 'It is still a very difficult conversation. As a military person, once you put that uniform on during your training, you are taught to be invincible and not to let anyone down.'

It is hard to think of a better example of what ten years in the Army had done for Harry than that speech and the sense of duty he clearly felt. Nor could onlookers believe that it was wayward Harry and not serious William who was showing how a Royal should behave. A highly chastened Prince William was out and about with Kate a few days later to honour the Irish Guards on St Patrick's Day, but the message was clear: Harry had grown up. And many people suggested it was Harry's relationship with a then-relatively unknown actress who had hastened the change. So just what had he and Meghan been up to since the news of their relationship had broken just six months previously?

CHAPTER 13

CHRISTMAS IN KENSINGTON

The news was out: Harry and Meghan Markle were officially a couple. There had been a great deal of interest in Harry's previous girlfriends, but it was as nothing compared to this. A biracial divorcee actress? It certainly wouldn't have been a possibility just a couple of decades previously. And yet the good feeling towards the two of them was palpable. Even before they knew anything much about Meghan, the British people wanted Harry to have his happy ending, and if this was who he wanted, then the feeling was that this was who he should have.

In many ways it was remarkable that the news took as long to break as it did. It turned out that the pair had actually met through a friend in May 2016 when Harry was in Toronto on business that was to do with the Invictus Games; he reportedly bombarded her with texts until she agreed to go out with him. Over the summer Meghan visited London – and given her beau's high profile and the fact that she was herself an actress it is remarkable that no one cottoned on to what was happening – and by August 2016, the two had solidly defined themselves as an item. More than that: they were said to be head over heels in love.

And so it all began: the two wearing matching bracelets; Meghan posting pictures on Instagram – Harry was one of her followers – of spooning bananas and bulldogs wearing the Union Jack flag; acres of press coverage about whether Harry could marry a divorcee (and remarkably little comment about the fact that his father had already done exactly that). Before much more was known about Meghan the pairing seemed extraordinary, but as details emerged of her charitable work, her love of travel, her strong personality and her encouragement of Harry, it became obvious that the two were an ideal match. First it emerged that Meghan had been at Balmoral for Harry's thirty-second birthday. Then it was reported that Harry had flown to Canada over Hallowe'en, where they went to a party, and Harry – safely behind a mask – trick or treated. The rest of the time was spent behind closed doors, cooking and playing with Meghan's dogs. It was his first trip to Toronto as Meghan's boyfriend and it was by all accounts a roaring success.

Of course now, however, there was a new consideration: everyone was desperate to see the two of them together. Harry appeared to be suffering from cold feet: in early November he had been planning on taking a trip to the Caribbean, possibly to meet up with his new love. At the last minute he changed his mind and decided not to go.

Of course not everyone was happy for the new couple and one of these, alas, was Meghan's older half-sister, Samantha Grant. Embarrassing relatives are nothing new in Royal circles – Kate Middleton's Uncle Gary was a case in point – but from the start, Samantha's gibes at Meghan merely provoked an outpouring of sympathy for the actress. Meghan was a 'social climber' who had 'always wanted to be a princess,' she claimed. Meghan's other half-sibling, Thomas Markle (who was to cause some embarrassment himself in January 2017), stepped in. 'I don't think the Royal family will have a problem with Meghan,' he said, and in that, at least, he was right.

Apart from her cryptic posting on Instagram, however, Meghan was proving she had what every Royal significant other needs: discretion. For a high-profile actress and human rights campaigner she was keeping remarkably quiet. But of course unlike Harry's previous amours, Meghan already knew what it was like to live life in the spotlight. She was no ingénue.

Her nephew, Tyler Dooley, however, was a little more indiscreet. 'You know how you can tell when someone really likes somebody by the excitement in their voice?' he told *The Sun*. 'All I can say is she is happy. She is very happy, and I am sure that is because of Harry. She seems very excited. She is going through a very positive phase of her life. She's open about the relationship to her friends and her dad. Meghan has mentioned Harry to me, but it is not something she is boasting about. I know Harry went over to Toronto, where they hung out together. And, of course, she plans to go to London when she wraps up filming in Canada this month. They are going to find a way to see each other.'

Speaking to the *Irish Sun on Sunday*, Tyler also revealed that Meghan had been rather hurt by the gibes from her half-sister Samantha. 'Meghan was hurt,' he said. 'She was stung by hearing the things my other aunt said about her. It left her shocked and concerned about her family. She could not believe it. You cannot climb the social ladder on the backs of anybody else. If you are a star in a TV show, of course you are going to be exposed to producers and celebrities. It is not social climbing, it is Hollywood. It's the entertainment business. She doesn't stop working. When you are around all of these people of course you're going to network.

'She has an energy about her that you just can't find,' he went on. 'There is nobody like Meghan. In terms of women, she is the best you can get. We have completely different jobs in completely different towns and we still keep in touch because she is a quality person.'

Harry clearly felt the same.

Speaking with the approval of Clarence House, former Royal butler Grant Harrold gave an interview to the *Daily Mirror*. 'Harry loves her and she loves him,' he said. 'And that will be what matters in the eyes of the Queen and Prince Charles. I don't see any reason why Meghan couldn't be The One. The royal family are a very modern family. Her past will not count against her. I've never seen any of the royals judge, either in private or in public. So what's to say Meghan is not right for Harry? I think Harry wants to get it right now. He wants to make absolutely sure she's The One. She will need to follow certain etiquette and be more careful how she behaves.'

Harrold explained that she would have been made welcome by the Royal family. 'They've been dating for a few months and she will have met all of the core people in Harry's family by now. Charles would have made her feel very welcome, like any father, and the Queen is wonderful at making people feel relaxed and comfortable. I've no doubt she'll do exactly the same for Meghan.'

Of course what all of this was doing simply served to whip up a renewed frenzy of interest in Meghan. It was in early November 2016 that Harry issued the statement mentioned in the first chapter of this book, pointing out that this was Meghan's life and not a game, but while many people very much sympathised with him, this also unwittingly served as a confirmation that yes, it really was a serious relationship. There was renewed excitement when, a couple of days later, it was reported that Meghan was flying to London to visit her boyfriend: by all accounts, she told the makers of *Suits* she had 'something important to do'. Not that they would have been complaining: *Suits* was receiving unprecedented publicity as the entire world raced to find out everything they could about the divine Miss M. There was particular satisfaction every time someone managed to unearth one of her love scenes. Not since the days of Koo Stark had the backstory of a Royal paramour allowed anyone to do that.

Against this backdrop of frenzied excitement Harry continued his Royal duties, joining the Duke of

Edinburgh at the Field of Remembrance to honour the war dead and exercising his usual ability to connect with everyone around him, in this case a six-year-old boy and his grandmother. The boy, Harrison Degiorgio-Lewis, had never known his Uncle Aaron Lewis, who had been killed in Afghanistan, but he was wearing the soldier's campaign medals and beret when he met the Prince: 'We remember Aaron every day and miss him every day,' his grandmother, Helen Lewis, related. 'It was lovely to speak to Prince Harry about Aaron. A charity set up in his memory is helping veterans that have been injured, both combat injuries and those with post-traumatic stress disorder. Our charity has even helped some of the guys that competed in Harry's Invictus Games and we were talking about that.'

Was it any surprise, on the back of that, that Harry's popularity continued to soar? A prince who had served in the military himself, including two missions in Afghanistan, now doing his bit for his fellow soldiers, both fallen and still with us, could scarcely have failed to have mopped up public adoration. And now it turned out that he was in love with a beautiful American actress, who could possibly have begrudged him that? The pair didn't appear in public together, but Meghan was spotted out shopping at the upmarket Whole Foods Market, a short walk from Kensington Palace, where Harry lived in Nottingham Cottage; a noted foodie and cook, there was happy speculation that she must have been cooking for him on their cosy nights in.

The visit was a whistlestop one and so by the time Harry attended a Twickenham rugby match to watch England play South Africa, he was sitting next to a different princess – Princess Charlene of Monaco. No matter. Everyone was still having a field day digging up chunks of Meghan's past and now came the revelation that a year previously *Hello! Canada* had asked her to pick between William and Harry during a quick-fire question and answer session: fortunately, in the circumstances, after some initial giggling she replied, 'Harry? Harry, sure.'

Harry's next concern was Meghan's safety: while with him she had the same protection that he did; alone, however, she was on her own. Reports surfaced that he was thinking of hiring a bodyguard: Meghan's reported response was that this was 'charming but unnecessary'. Harry's concern, given what had happened to his mother, was deemed to be understandable, if excessive – and only endeared him to the rest of the country even more.

Matters were briefly put on hold when Harry jetted off to Antigua for a two-week trip around the Caribbean to represent the Queen, but any hopes that the romance would enjoy a lower profile were dashed from almost the moment the Prince touched down. Antigua's prime minister, Gaston Browne, lost no time in inviting Harry to spend his honeymoon on the island: 'I understand that there may be a new addition to the Royal family very soon,' he began. 'I am told that there may be a princess and I just want to say that should you make the decision to honeymoon, then Antigua and Barbuda want to welcome you. We have been voted consistently as the best honeymoon destination in the Caribbean and one of the best in the world, so there will be nowhere in the world as special to spend your honeymoon, when that day arrives.'

Harry, looking hideously embarrassed, did not meet his eye.

It was in any case a poignant visit: as a child, Harry had visited nearby Barbuda with his mother and told companions he was coming back soon, although he did not specify with whom. He went on to cavort with dancers in traditional dress and filleted his own fish in St Kitts, before moving on to St Vincent on the Royal Navy's *Wave Knight* ship, when he was again put in a difficult position when forced to observe silence for the Cuban leader Fidel Castro, who had just died. Again, plainly embarrassed, he did as his hosts asked, although there were some sharp words back in the UK for those who had allowed him to be ambushed in such a way.

Next up was Grenada, while back in the UK William was drawn into the mix as he angrily denied reports he disapproved of his brother's relationship and fully supported the statement that had been issued. Meanwhile, in the Caribbean, the tour was continuing beautifully despite the embarrassing situations in which he had found himself – and which he was deemed to have handled very well. This, after all, was the kind of activity that awaited him over the decades to come: as a senior Royal, Harry would be expected to represent his family and country, and he was thought to be doing a pretty good job. 'It's a very different tour for him, doing a lot of things on behalf of the Queen with many more formal bits,' said one of the courtiers who was travelling with him. 'But so far it has exceeded his expectations about what he thought was possible.'

After a fairly gruelling two weeks Harry was due back for more official events in the UK but took a 1,700-mile detour to see Meghan during an extremely brief stopover in Canada on his way home. 'He was due to fly back to London with the rest of his entourage but he changed his mind because they couldn't bear to be apart,' a friend told *The Sun*. 'It's a very short stopover as he has a charity appearance in London tomorrow. It's just another sign of how head over heels he is. We've never seen him so happy.' But still he was sticking to his duties: after the briefest of breaks Harry was back in London to attend an ICAP fundraising event for Sentebale. But there was no doubt in anyone's mind as to how serious the relationship was now.

Harry's growing serious side was underlined in a documentary due to come out at Christmas about his work with Sentebale. 'The film is also rather revealing about who he is and where he is in life. He talks candidly about the past, the present and his own future,' said host Tom Bradby, an ITV newsreader who was close to both princes. 'But mostly he talks about how fired up he is about his position and what he can do with it. There is, he says, too much focus on the bad news in life. It's great to be good, he tells us, and boring to be bad.'

Could it be Meghan who was bringing out this maturity? The growing seriousness of their relationship was brought home again when she was pictured wearing a necklace with the initials M and H, and shortly afterwards, a couple of weeks before Christmas, Meghan was back in London. There was no question of her being invited to join the Royal family at their traditional Christmas celebration at Sandringham – they were not actually engaged and that is usually the status required before the invite goes out – but it appeared that the couple had opted to celebrate it on their own.

They were seen buying a Christmas tree from Pines and Needles in London (the staff gave them some mistletoe) much to the astonishment of the workers in the shop: 'You could have heard a pin drop, or a needle, when Prince Harry and Meghan walked in,' shopkeeper Sam Lyle told the *Daily Mirror*. 'They were both completely charming together, blissfully unaware that our jaws had hit the floor.'

Ollie Wilkinson, who also worked in the shop, commented, 'They went to pay and Harry also donated some money to charity. I then handed them a bunch of mistletoe and Meghan said she loved it. Harry walked off with the tree on his left shoulder, holding Meghan's hand with his right hand, while she held the mistletoe.'

The documentary about Sentebale was duly shown, in December, in which Harry was seen to be explaining that he had accepted who he was and had found his niche. His work with the charity was credited with having helped with that. 'For me personally it's an escape, but not only have I found an escape, I've found a way of using the name and the position for good,' he said. 'There's a lot of unfinished work that my mother never completed. I'm not suggesting that either of us is going to take over that mantle, but naturally there's a crossover of those passions between myself and William that the two of us share with what my mother started. I have this love of Africa that will never disappear. And I hope it carries on with my children as well.'

Harry wasn't the only one thinking about children. Meghan's nephew Tyler Dooley popped up again: it wasn't clear if he had received official permission to speak out, but, as ever, his intervention only served to heighten interest in the couple. 'She's achieved success in her career and now she's found Mr Right. A family is next,' he told an Australian magazine in the wake of Meghan's return to Canada. 'She has said she wants to have kids and she would be a good wife and mother. She had a mothering side even as a young girl – she's a natural and it's the right time for her to have a family. Meghan has always been very caring. I look up to her now, just like I did when I was a kid. Meghan emailed when the news about her and Prince Harry hit the headlines. She said she was very excited, very happy and content. You could really tell she was in a good place.'

Back in the UK a few days later, after being seen eating out around London and attending the theatre, where the couple saw *The Curious Incident of the Dog in the Night-Time*, Meghan flew out of London and

Harry's immediate melancholic demeanour signalled that Christmas at Sandringham was not going to be quite as much fun as usual that year. He, alongside five protection staff, personally escorted Meghan to Heathrow, before putting in a rather forlorn appearance at a party for Heads Together, an umbrella group that he, William and Kate had set up for eight mental-health charities. He was clearly missing his beloved.

But he brightened up for Christmas Day itself. William and Kate were not at Sandringham, having opted to stay with her parents instead, and on the traditional Christmas Day church outing, giving rise to some alarm, the Queen was absent, too. It was most unlike this most dutiful of monarchs, who was said to be suffering from a heavy cold; in the event she was not seen in public for some time, causing a good deal of national anxiety before appearing on the national stage again. But most of the other senior Royals were there, including Harry: laughing and joking, he was the centre of attention, even if his heart was clearly elsewhere.

A few days after Christmas, Meghan was pictured attending a yoga class in Toronto with her mother, Doria; back in London it was reported that Harry had overtaken William in the Royal duty stakes, carrying out eighty-six days of appointments compared with William's eighty (although of course William was still working as a helicopter pilot). Harry was the most well-travelled Royal that year as well, clocking up 61,800 miles of overseas public engagements. More than ever he was doing his bit for The Firm.

Another member of Meghan's family popped up to share what was going on: her half-brother Thomas, speaking to MailOnline. It was not clear whether Meghan had met Harry's father, but he had certainly met hers, another sign of quite how serious it was all turning out to be. 'My dad knew about [the relationship] from the start,' Thomas said. 'He first met Prince Harry about six months ago in Toronto. He goes once every couple of months – [Meghan and her father] are very close and they stay in close contact. He's pretty happy about Harry and he's extremely proud of her. They have an amazing relationship, they're very close and they always have been.'

And while there had been many reports about how besotted Harry was, it seemed Meghan felt exactly the same. 'She's very much in love and she's obviously happy because if she wasn't happy, she wouldn't be there,' Thomas went on. 'So she is happy and [the relationship is] taking off, which is good, and I wish them all the best. I couldn't be happier for her. I think it is wonderful. As long as he takes care of and loves Meg, he doesn't have to do anything else [...] he looks like a genuinely good man – and he was in the services as well. He looks happy, he looks like he's stress-free and like he could be a good guy for Meg. They get along and that's what matters [...] Prince Harry is lucky. She's the right girl for the job [of being a princess]. It's not a job but she's the right girl. You couldn't get a more refined, well-rounded person than her. Look at them when they look at each other – they love each other. So it'll be great, it'll be royal. I just want her to be happy. I would like to shake his hand and meet him.'

It was pretty effusive stuff, but the more the relationship came under the spotlight, the more obvious it became quite how serious it all was. They weren't apart for long: there were reports that they spoke at least twice a day on FaceTime, and Meghan made it back to London for the New Year; shortly afterwards Harry whisked her off to Norway to see the Northern Lights. The couple jetted into Tromsø and rented a cabin in the fjords for a week on the edge of the Arctic Circle, during a period that was prime-time viewing for Aurora Borealis. Inge Solheim – known as 'The Ice Ninja' – who had been with Harry during polar explorations and the Walking With The Wounded charity, had arranged the trip. Whale watching and trips on the fjords were all on the agenda.

It was their first proper holiday together, a testing time for any couple, and one they passed with flying colours. There was also the fact that, now they were established, Meghan's life had begun to change and not simply in the way anyone else's does when they have found a new match. Security considerations really were becoming a concern, not least because Meghan, like Harry, was an active campaigner for charity, which meant she travelled to remote places. Perhaps there might have to be a rethink on that. And while the makers of *Suits* were giving every indication of being desperate to sign her up for all eternity, it was not clear what Meghan herself thought about that.

The last time there had been such a public romance between a prince and an actress had been over half a century earlier, when Prince Rainier of Monaco made Grace Kelly his princess. Could it be about to happen again? And Grace, of course, had had to give up her illustrious Hollywood career in the course of her romance, although admittedly her husband was the ruler of his country, which was not the case with Harry. So just what was going to happen next?

CHAPTER 14

THE PITFALLS
OF FAME

That Meghan's profile had soared due to her relationship with Harry was in no doubt, and in January 2017 it was highlighted in one of those nonsense polls that mean everything and nothing: she came top of a poll to find the world's most alluring eyes. It was one of those bits of trivia that amused, but while on the whole meaningless, the very fact that someone most people in the UK hadn't had a clue about a year earlier had pushed the Duchess of Cambridge, no less, into third place spoke volumes in itself.

But an increased profile has a downside, as Meghan was shortly to find out. Many people, including the

Middleton family, had found themselves embarrassed by a relative and now it was Meghan's turn: it made headlines around the world when her half-brother Thomas was arrested for holding a gun to a woman called Darlene Blunt's head in an attempt to get her to leave his house. Even more embarrassingly, a very dishevelled-looking mugshot also beamed all over the globe.

The timing was not good: the arrest happened around the same time that Meghan was introduced to Harry's sister-in-law Kate and her little daughter Charlotte. Everyone was well aware of how awkward this was, not least Thomas himself: 'I am incredibly sorry for my actions and I'm especially sorry to everyone affected by my drinking,' he said in a statement. 'I am seeking help and I promise I will be the best person I can be going forward. Thank you for understanding.'

His ever-helpful son Tyler stepped in: 'He knows it is an embarrassment to Meghan and the family,' he told *The Sun*. 'He is very sorry and is apologising to everyone. He just needs some time to heal and reflect on life. But he wants to apologise for everything. He is in the spotlight now and everyone gets to see his flaws. Due to being inebriated, his emotions got the better of him and he got into an argument with his girlfriend. He's not like this normally. I also want to apologise on behalf of my dad.

Unfortunately my father has a problem with alcohol. He is now in recovery.'

Kate was no doubt sympathetic: she had had her own issues in the past with her Uncle Gary (called the 'black sheep' of the family, he was a self-made millionaire with a reportedly dodgy past connected to drugs and crime). Meanwhile the publicity was doing Meghan's career no harm at all: the channel Dave showed pictures of her in a wedding dress, as part of a trailer: 'They're almost royalty' the caption said. Thomas was taking on board the full implications of what he had done: 'Everyone makes mistakes,' he said. 'This time I made a bad one. But we all do. If I may say so, Prince Harry has made a few in his time and learnt from them. I just need the same chance. Marriage and kids is on the cards for Meghan and Harry and I still want to go to the wedding if they'll let me.'

Darlene Blunt, who by all accounts was now somewhat regretting calling the police and wanted to patch things up with her beau, said the same: 'I've always been a fan of Harry,' she said. 'I would love to meet the Royals. I'd buy the prettiest dress if Tom and I can go to the wedding.'

Possibly least said, soonest mended, and in any case, Meghan was getting on with business as usual. She flew to India to help promote women's health and hygiene in Delhi on behalf of World Vision Canada; in the course of it she had her hands painted with henna, much to the delight of the press. She had been doing this kind of work for some time – but this was before she caught the eye of a prince and one whose own mother had been famed for her charitable work, at that. It was inevitable that comparisons were drawn with Princess Diana and inevitable too that people realised how much that must have appealed to Harry. And of course he too was strongly committed to his own charitable work. But it was rumoured that the trip had been cut from ten days to five; those security fears were ever present. Harry's earlier offer to hire a bodyguard was not looking so over the top now.

Meghan's changed status was apparent in almost every aspect of her life now. When the actor Patrick Adams, who played Meghan/Rachel's onscreen love Mike Ross in *Suits*, took part in a question and answer about the show, he was asked, 'Hey Patrick! What's it like making out on-screen with the potentially future princess of England?'

'The same as it was before she was potentially a future princess of England,' said Patrick, thus unwittingly of course boosting speculation that Meghan really was just that. And the frenzy was ramped up higher still when in early February 2017 the two of them were seen in public together for the first time when Meghan paid a visit to London. Amid rumours that they were by now 'practically living together', they were spotted holding hands after a private dinner at Soho House…

Meanwhile, Meghan was pictured carrying a bunch of flowers to Harry's Kensington Palace home; she was also seen wearing a ring that appeared to be decorated with the letter H. Previously she had been sporting a necklace with the letters M and H; now there was speculation that this was a 'promise ring' signalling an engagement lay ahead. An engagement expert was wheeled out to back this up: 'It means, "I'm here for the long haul", and I think we can probably expect this to lead on to the main event,' George Watts, of the Wedding Fairy consultancy, told the *Daily Mirror*. 'This is a really thought-out ring. I think it's Prince Harry saying: "I'm serious about this girl and going to do it my way".'

Reports surfaced that the couple had visited William and Kate's Norfolk home and that Meghan met young Prince George as well: 'Harry took Meghan up to Anmer Hall on a secret mission to meet more of the VIPs in his life – George and Charlotte,' a Royal insider told the *Daily Star Sunday*. 'They all had tea and biscuits, and took a walk in the grounds with the dogs. Meghan was totally taken with the children. She was playing with them, mucking around and did silly voices and impressions.

Pictures surfaced on Instagram of Meghan's Toronto pad: a symphony in white on white, marble, modern furniture and nice artwork, it garnered sympathetic comment that she clearly had the tastes befitting the girlfriend of a prince. Her own blog also revealed quite a few gems: as 14 February approached she posted: 'I'm a real sucker for Valentine's Day. I wake up every February 14 waiting with bated breath to be dipped into a kiss'. The ideal gifts that year were a white lace bra and knickers (surely Meghan must have realised what reaction that would provoke), a bottle of cologne, a luggage label and 'love coupons' which offered romantic favours. Make of that what you will.

And needless to say, observers did. Meghan's blog had become a source of amusement for some, in much the same way that Pippa Middleton's advice on entertaining had; some people were in fact fond of comparing the two women's nuggets of advice. Meghan came in for some criticism for publishing a playlist guaranteed to beat the winter blues: 'When the air is filled with positive vibes, there is no winter cold that can block out the warmth of happy hearts.' Nor did her advice to drink 'golden milk' (warm milk with ginger and turmeric) go down well with everyone. And indeed, perhaps as a precursor to a future Royal life, in early April 2017 came the news that The

Tig was shutting down – on the landing page there was only a heartfelt note written by Meghan herself on the site thanking her fans and telling them to 'keep finding those Tig moments of discovery, keep laughing and taking risks, and keep being "the change you wish to see in the world".' To many, it was a surefire signal that both her relationship with Harry and within the royal family were becoming more official.

Indeed, the surest sign that things were getting serious between the pair came when both Harry and Meghan were invited to the wedding of Tom 'Skippy' Inskip and Lara Hughes-Young at Round Hill Hotel in Montego Bay, Jamaica, where Harry was to be best man. (Harry flew in on economy; Meghan arrived in a friend's borrowed private jet, which caused some amusement to onlookers.) They had been apart for a couple of weeks and were happy for a romantic reunion to take place in full view of the cameras: staying at a six-bedroom villa with a private pool (cost: £14,000 for the minimum three-night stay), the two embraced publicly. Harry sported lime green shorts and Meghan a turquoise bikini: by this time it was clear that neither cared what anyone thought and that they would carry on as they chose. Nor did anyone seem unduly concerned that this was in fact the country where Meghan had married for the first time; if anything it added a frisson that she was there with her new beau.

The trip was a big success. The wedding celebrations lasted three days: Harry was an usher at the ceremony itself, which took place at Hopewell Baptist Church. Meghan was seen to be happily socialising with fellow guests: she had met a number of them before and was said to have formed particular friendships with Lara and Lizzy Wilson, who was married to Guy Pelly. Dressed in a floor-length number by Erdem (coincidentally, the Duchess of Cambridge had worn the same designer at a Buckingham Palace reception that week), Meghan was clearly at ease in the crowd. 'Meghan has got to know Harry's inner circle well and she has got close to Lara, Skippy's wife, and Lizzy, Guy's wife, who was really looking out for her,' a friend told *Vanity Fair*. 'In truth it took a bit of time for them to all get to know each other, and there was a bit of a cultural divide at first. Skippy and co. have a rather unique and often rude sense of humour. If you don't know them they can be a bit crude and rather brash with a rather silly sense of toilet humour. It took Meghan a while to get used to them and vice versa, but they have really warmed to her. They do joke about some of her New Age philosophies though.'

It was a thoroughly good-humoured affair. Harry's

aunt, Sarah, Duchess of York, was there with her daughter Eugenie, and at the reception afterwards, Harry was said to have demonstrated his dancing skills by attempting to moonwalk à la Michael Jackson and accidentally bumping into a waitress and sending a tray of drinks flying. The poor boy was said to be mortified but the waitress and the rest of the guests were only too happy to laugh it off.

Weddings are, naturally, times at which attached but not yet engaged guests become the subject of a good deal of teasing and speculation. This was certainly the case here, with a lot of fellow guests telling Meghan and Harry that they would be next down the aisle. 'This is the first time Harry has shown her off so publicly by taking her to a friend's wedding,' a friend told *The Sun*. 'She's met his mates before, but this is different. It's a really significant step. Skippy's one of his last mates to marry and Harry is best man. So it's natural he'd want Meg on his arm. It's only a matter of time before they're next. They've discussed it and she's ready to leave acting for him. This latest series of *Suits* will be her last and she wants to do more charity work. That's why Harry loves her so much. She's smart, sassy and wants to use her position for good.'

He also wanted to give Meghan a treat. The Windsor boys clearly know how to treat the women in their life:

when they were courting, William was forever whisking Kate off on exotic holidays and now Harry did likewise. While in situ in Jamaica, they reportedly went on to stay at a beautiful hotel called The Caves, which did indeed have caves built into the rocks, lit up with candles and serving up Jamaican specialities including sweet potato mash, saltfish and fried banana. It was an extremely private location, giving the two of them a chance to be together away from prying eyes.

Inevitably, this ramped up speculation that there would soon be an engagement announcement of their own; the rumour mill went into overdrive when it emerged that No. 10 had made it known that a Saturday wedding would be preferable, to avoid the need for a bank holiday. Meghan's use of social media had noticeably declined; there were no more spooning bananas or dogs wearing the Union Jack flag, almost certainly due to the Palace's and Harry's wish to conduct his life in private. Meghan herself was now beginning to see the downside of sharing too much: 'The media fascination really shocked her,' said a friend. 'Initially she enjoyed the attention. She smiled for photographers and did cheeky things like [in December] wear that necklace with an M and H initial on it. She posted knowing captions on Instagram and got to meet Prince Charles, Prince William and Kate, which was all very exciting.' But as with so many Royal girlfriends before her, Meghan realised that discretion was the order of the day.

Her co-stars were well aware of the change in her life. 'I'm super excited for her,' said Patrick Adams. 'As you can imagine, it is a massive deal, obviously, if you hadn't noticed. I didn't wanna get involved. I just wanted to say, "I love you, I support you, I hope you're happy. You seem really happy", and if she ever needed anybody to talk to in the madness – 'cause it is madness, it's madness what the world puts somebody through when they're going through this process. But if there's anyone in the world who is designed to be able to deal with it and deal with it professionally, it's Meghan Markle.'

The only potential obstacle was seen to be the Queen, although it was hard to see what objection she could raise – Harry was now some way down the line of succession, on top of which it was said in Royal circles that she was pleased to see Harry happier than he had seemed in years.

But as ever the two had to part: Meghan was soon spotted back in snowy Toronto carrying her yoga mat; Harry, accompanied by his aunt, Princess Anne, was seen at an England/Scotland rugby match. The long-distance relationship, with its constant Atlantic-hopping, went on. However, while its seriousness was no longer in doubt, another issue came up: Harry's (and thus Meghan's) future title. When Royal sons married they were given further titles – Prince Andrew became the Duke of York on his wedding, and Prince Edward the Earl of Wessex. Marlene Koenig, of the blog Royal Musings, believed she had an inside track: 'Most likely, he will be created a Duke,' she said. Meghan would thus be HRH The Duchess of Sussex.

'Her rank would be a princess by marriage of the United Kingdom, Great Britain and Northern Ireland,' Marlene continued. 'If Harry marries during the Queen's lifetime, his children will not be Royal until his father is King due to the 1917 Letters Patent. Sussex would be a good choice for Harry – only one before him – a prince who married for love twice and did not care about the formality of his father's marital law.' She was referring to the only previous Duke of Sussex, Prince Augustus Frederick, one of George III's sons and an uncle of Queen Victoria, who died in 1843, since when the title had been dormant. The Duke married twice, both times for love, interestingly enough, but neither marriage was legal under English law and so the title was not passed down to his own heir.

In the meantime, Meghan continued her own charity work, speaking out on International Women's Day about the plight of women who have to cope with the stigma surrounding menstruation, specifically problems she had seen when she was in India. 'To remedy this problem, young girls need access to toilets, and at a most basic level, sanitary pads,' she wrote in *Time* magazine, and in addressing an issue with which some people felt uncomfortable, there were clear shades of Princess Diana. Meghan was also pictured wearing a bindi on her forehead, just as Diana had done in 1992. She was inspiring to women in other ways, too – it was reported that the number of women studying law had risen as a direct result of watching her as Rachel Zane in *Suits*.

Scarcely a week had passed before Meghan was back in London, this time being treated to an after-hours visit to London's Natural History Museum. 'Meg had always wanted to go, so Harry arranged a private visit,' a friend told *The Sun*. 'It's quite romantic after dark as all the exhibits, including the dinosaurs, are all still lit up. And of course, they had it to themselves.'

Then of course Meghan was spotted cheering on Harry as he played polo at the Audi Polo Challenge at Coworth Park Polo Club in Ascot in early May 2017 just days before Meghan's somewhat secretive appearance as Harry's guest at the evening reception of Pippa Middleton's wedding to financier James Matthews in Berkshire on May 20th – the surest sign possible to the world that Meghan is here to stay. It was thought the couple wanted to spend as much time as they could together before Meghan's filming commitments kicked in over the spring and summer, although there was an increasing amount of talk about her giving up acting altogether. After all, the flitting back and forth across the Atlantic simply was not sustainable for the longer term.

And indeed, a report soon surfaced on E! Online that Meghan was thinking along those lines herself. Something had to give and it would have to come from her side. Harry could not stop being a member of the Royal family and Royals such as the Duke of Windsor who were perceived to have walked away from their responsibilities generally tended to have an unfulfilling life. It was not unknown, however, for actresses to give up acting if a tiara was in the offing: the most famous example of course was Princess Grace. And so it emerged that Meghan was 'ready to be done with *Suits* [and] acting in general,' a source told E! News. 'Even before Harry, she was starting to think about transitioning out of acting. She wants to focus on other worldly endeavours she is passionate about, like her philanthropy.'

Again there were strong echoes of Princess Diana. This was also taken as further proof that the couple were ready to settle down, with speculation about when Harry might propose. Meghan shared a birthday – 4 August – with Harry's Great-Grandmother, the late Queen Mother, so that was one obvious option. As always in Royal circles, however, the considerations went far beyond what would suit the happy couple themselves. The Queen and Prince Philip were due to celebrate their seventieth wedding anniversary in the course of 2017, which meant that nothing would be allowed to overshadow it. An engagement would be acceptable but the wedding itself would not.

Meghan continued to keep her head down. She had started to appear less communicable these days, not least because like anyone connected to the Royal family, she had to be a lot more cautious about what she could say and to whom. She was 'just keeping a super low profile right now,' a source told E! News. 'Meghan is the darling of Toronto. Locals love her so much and she really engaged herself into the community when she moved here for *Suits* years ago. The city basically adopted her and she fits right in. She's just not as accessible now but she's always been so kind and genuinely so sweet to people around town.'

So would she make the move and give up her career? When Prince Charles and Princess Diana first got married, their combined star power was like no other; they appeared to complement one another perfectly. In fact, the opposite was the case. With Harry and Meghan, however, despite their very disparate backgrounds, they clearly had a huge amount in common – and together were taking the world by storm.

CHAPTER 15

HAPPY EVER AFTER?

There had never been a Royal romance like Harry and Meghan's: Meghan was divorced, biracial, an actress who had taken part in some steamy love scenes and about as far removed from European royalty, British aristocracy and even the Home Counties as it was possible to get. She was also a perfect match for Harry, with not only a great deal in common but with a nurturing side that anyone who had lost their mother when they were just 12 years old would need. A generation previously their union would have been unthinkable but the world had changed and the Windsors had changed with it. And strangely enough, it was Harry's mother who was partly responsible for that. No one wanted a Royal bride just on the grounds that she ticked a number of boxes ever again.

But whatever her future status, Meghan was not about to let anyone forget her ethnic roots. She spoke of her anger at being airbrushed, ostensibly to get rid of her freckles, but with the effect of making her look whiter. 'To this day, my pet peeve is when my skin tone is changed and my freckles are airbrushed out,' she told *Allure* magazine. 'For castings, I was labelled "ethnically ambiguous". Was I Latina? Sephardic? Exotic Caucasian? Add the freckles to the mix and it created quite the conundrum.' It was only African American studies that made her take a new look at these issues: 'It was the first time I could put a name to feeling too light in the black community, too mixed in the white community,' she said.

Meanwhile, Harry was having issues of his own. In the wake of his brother's disastrous trip to Verbier, when he was pictured partying while most of the rest of the Royal family celebrated Commonwealth Day, Harry had to cancel a planned trip of his own. A big party had been in the offing, but given the negative publicity surrounding William's jaunt, it was deemed considerably wiser to stay in situ in London, although the consolation was that Meghan was there. Elsewhere however, it was business as usual – Harry sent a video message wishing Sir Elton

John a happy birthday on the occasion of the pop star's seventieth bash, and found himself on a list of men of the year put forward by the brand Lynx.

In all it had been an astonishing transformation for the two of them. Harry had been the hot headed young prince a little too fond of falling out of nightclubs in his youth, but who had matured beyond anyone's expectations to the extent that he was now viewed as one of the major assets of the Royal family. Meghan, meanwhile, had been a little known actress from a somewhat troubled family background who, even before Harry, had metamorphosed into an on-screen success who used her profile to help others less fortunate than herself. Remind you of anyone? The parallels with Diana were clear.

There were other indications of the changes in both of them. In Harry's case it was an increased maturity; in Meghan's it was a change of personal style. Her image had previously been very much that of the Hollywood glamour puss, with flesh on display where needed, but her appearance was becoming sleeker, more sophisticated and in the eyes of some people at least, increasingly reflective of the Duchess of Cambridge. It certainly was more regal than had previously been the case.

'Meghan's style has always been quite feminine slightly sexy, yet we have been seeing a much more polished and tailored version of late,' style expert Naomi Isted, Express.co.uk. 'Meghan's recent looks are sleeker just as we saw Kate's style evolve into much more tailored and chic looks, Meghan seems to be following suit. They have very similar body types and naturally as the relationship grows so will her wardrobe into a very defined look just as Kate's has become super sleek, tailored and every inch the modern day princess.'

Of course before she became a modern day princess there was another minor matter to overcome – that by law, before he married, Harry had to get the permission of the Queen. It was not widely understood that the Royal Marriages Act 1772 meant that the monarch was able to veto the marriage of a member of her family and is also called upon to give formal consent to any family marriages in order to guard against those that could 'diminish the status of the royal house'. This had nothing at all to do with Meghan's racial background but it could have applied to her status as a divorcee, although given that three of the Queen's children were divorcees and two of them had remarried meant that it was almost inconceivable this would be the case.

And indeed, matters had become more liberal. At one stage all Royals needed the consent of the monarch before they could wed but in 2013 that was slimmed down to

Prince Charles, Prince William, Prince George, Princess Charlotte, Prince Harry, and Prince Andrew. Position in the line to inherit the throne and so after William and Kate's daughter Charlotte was born in May 2015, Princess Beatrice became seventh in line and Eugenie eighth, giving them free choice.

But it still applied to the more senior Royals and it would to Harry. Prince William had to get the Queen's consent before he proposed to Kate: 'Our Most Dearly Beloved Grandson Prince William Arthur Philip Louis of Wales, K.G. and Our Trusty and Well-beloved Catherine Elizabeth Middleton,' were indeed allowed to get engaged. Harry would have to do the same but the reality was that the Queen would never have denied him the permission he wanted. Harry and Meghan's relationship spoke volumes about the change in the Royal family – which had faced a serious crisis less than a century previously when another prince fell in love with an American divorcee – and even in the country at large. The fact that the vast majority of his grandmother's subjects barely raised an eyebrow at the news – apart from exhibiting a good deal of curiosity – showed quite how much society had changed.

There were also those who noticed a change in Harry's own personal appearance. Like William, he had always adopted the Sloane uniform of suits for business and chinos for more casual wear, but some observers remarked that his wardrobe was adopting somewhat earthier tones. 'Looking at Harry's style over the past year or so, it's clear that his relationship with Megan has had an influence on his personal style,' stylist Natalie Robinson told MailOnline. 'As sometimes happens when you spend a lot of time with someone, Harry has upped his colour game. He's introduced a range of lighter tones to his wardrobe, similar to Meghan's own style, which has undoubtedly given him a more contemporary, dapper image.'

Another plus was that unlike Harry's previous girlfriends, Meghan was actually used to being in the public eye. 'I imagine Meghan has better coping skills than someone who is just thrown into the spotlight,' Hilda Burke, a psychotherapist and life coach told *Hello* magazine. 'But she and Harry probably have to screen out what other people are saying and predicting for them. If you get caught in anyone else's opinion of your relationship, whether it's the mums at the school gate or the international media, I think you've lost your focus.'

Royal biographer Penny Junor also spoke to *Hello*: 'For someone who isn't used to being in the spotlight, suddenly having the attention of the world's press is terrifying. It's a huge plus that Meghan is used to that – it really makes a different. She's pretty chilled about it all.'

The rumours surrounding the relationship continued to swirl; the pair continued to fascinate. But perhaps more important than anything else was the fact that Harry was so patently obviously happy. The Royals had always been told to put duty before happiness, but it was actually possible to combine the two, as Harry's own paternal grandparents had shown. William had been permitted to look beyond the usual stock of aristocrats and princesses and he, too, had achieved a clear contentment in his marriage that so many members of his family had not.

It was in the spring of 2017 that clear indications began to emerge that Meghan was preparing for a huge change in her circumstances. She closed The Tig, her lifestyle website, something that would have been no earthly reason to do were she not moving into a world where she could not be seen to be promoting something that might have commercial considerations. It was done in a very Meghan-like way: 'After close to three beautiful years on this adventure with you, it's time to say goodbye to The Tig,' she posted. 'What began as a passion project (my little engine that could) evolved into an amazing community of inspiration, support, fun and frivolity. You've made my days brighter and filled this experience with so much joy…. Thank you for everything.' It sounded a lot like a wrap for that particular stage of her life.

A very much more public affirmation of the growing closeness of their relationship came in September during the Invictus Games in Toronto. This was of course a cause very close to Harry's heart and he seemed determined to make it an almost official way of announcing that the relationship was a very serious one, but least as it was their first proper public appearance together. They sat apart at the opening ceremony of the games, but that was certainly not the case at the closing one. Harry left his official seat and went to the area where Meghan was sitting with her mother in the Air Canada Centre, along with Jessica Mulroney, daughter-in-law of the former Canadian prime minister Brian Mulroney and Meghan's friend Markus Anderson. The two were openly kissing and cuddling, which would in itself be enough to bring home the seriousness of their involvement, but given that Meghan's mother was also present seemed to carry even more weight.

A few weeks after that it was rumoured that Meghan had quit *Suits*. 'Meghan knows that she can't really act at the same time as being a princess and is happy to make this career sacrifice,' a source told the media. 'She really enjoys her charity work with Unicef and will broaden out her charity commitments when she becomes a full time royal.' Even though there had been no official announcement that she was leaving, the signs were there: Meghan's body double of the previous two years, Nicky Bursic, posted a picture of the two of them on Instagram, with the message, 'It's been an absolute pleasure and honour being your 'stand-in' for the last 2 years. Though I've been on @suits_usa for 6 years, the latter 2 has been my most memorable. Wishing you all the happiness in the world, Bella.' The added hashtag, #youdeserveitall, spoke for itself.

More and more details emerged and as November drew on, it became a feeding frenzy. It was reported that Meghan had moved in to Nottingham Cottage. Her dogs, Guy and Bogart, relocated to London, too. It was known that she had met the Queen in October when she and Harry turned up for afternoon tea and then, a clear sign that something was afoot, Ladbrokes stopped taking bets on the year of the Royal wedding. And then, of course, came the engagement.

Harry, the little lost boy, had become a mature man with a concern for people who were less fortunate than him and a determination to make his way in the world.

Meghan was a woman of substance. Yes, she was lucky to have found her prince. But he was every bit as lucky to have found his princess.